Tuticorin

Tuticorin

Adventures in Tamil Nadu's Crime Capital

V. Sudarshan

JUGGERNAUT BOOKS
C-I-128, First Floor, Sangam Vihar, Near Holi Chowk,
New Delhi 110080, India

First published by Juggernaut Books 2022

10 9 8 7 6 5 4 3 2 1

P-ISBN: 9789393986030
E-ISBN: 9789393986412

Typeset in Adobe Caslon Pro by R. Ajith Kumar, Noida

Printed at Nutech Print Services - India

For Kamakshi Vanchinathan, my mother,
without whom this and much more – all of it –
clearly wouldn't have been possible

Contents

Sketch Map of Tuticorin District

Courtesy: Rudraa Abirami Sudarshan

Preface

Tuticorin, or Thoothukudi as it is called now, is one of the most violent districts in Tamil Nadu. Situated along the picturesque coast of the Gulf of Mannar, it is awash with illicit liquor and populated with fiercely independent fisherfolk and farmers. It is infamous for its smugglers, gangsters and rowdies, particularly in and around the two harbours of the town, and a difficult district to handle for the police.

This large district, once a part of Tirunelveli, has witnessed unspeakable levels of violence, some undoubtedly due to the heavy-handedness of the police. In Kodiyankulam in 1995, eighteen people died after a force of six hundred uniformed men were deployed in the village, and more recently in May 2018, over a dozen died in police action in Thoothukudi.

So bad was the reputation, that in the seventies and eighties, it was said that if a lodger went looking for a room in Madras to stay in and gave a Tuticorin address, lodgekeepers invariably had second thoughts.

The stories that you will read here are all true. They are centred around the experiences of an idealistic young Indian Police Service (IPS) officer, Anoop Jaiswal, who retired as the director general of police (DGP), and was considered a misfit in the larger system. All the incidents you will read about occurred between January 1981, when Jaiswal joined the Police Academy with stars in his eyes, and 1989, when his posting in Tuticorin ended.

The narrative trails him as he grew into his job and adjusted to the reality of maintaining law and order in a difficult district, just as reality adjusted to his unconventional self. It chronicles Jaiswal's story as he found himself in the middle of a massacre, encountering murderers, kidnappers, thieves, sex workers, illicit liquor sellers, and rapacious moneylenders. All this as he came to grips with his accidental calling, and became a superintendent of police (SP) in the newly created district of Tuticorin.

Before we proceed, it would be useful to contextualize how Jaiswal's formative experiences as a cadet officer had crystallized in him, not only his single-minded determination to see justice served but also to reveal his strength of character and his singular dedication.

We will learn more about him in the following pages and the reader might be surprised that he ended up becoming a policeman, when he had actually wanted to be a scientist and had almost become a fighter pilot.

Jaiswal was born on 23 June 1955, in Gorakhpur, UP, into a humble family. He passed the UPSC civil services exam in 1980 and was offered a post in the IPS. By then, he was married to Neelam and had reported to the National Police Academy (NPA) in Hyderabad in January 1981 for training, after the obligatory stint at the Lal Bahadur Shastri Academy in September 1980.

As a cadet officer, Jaiswal had been thrown out of the NPA in Hyderabad, a very rare occurrence, and was allotted the Tamil Nadu cadre, almost on the eve of passing out. This was essentially as punishment for merely being unconventional and questioning the system during training.

With his second child already on the way, he had sought justice in the courts. What followed had been a lonely battle to clear his name. The Delhi High Court had dismissed his claim, and he had then appealed to the Supreme Court. Eventually, he had won his job back after more than two and a half years of court hearings. The Supreme Court judgement (*Anoop Jaiswal vs Government of India & Anr on 24 January, 1984*) is a landmark one, cited in the All India Reporter (1984 AIR 636, 1984 SCR (2) 453).

That was a turning point in his life.

I first met Anoop Jaiswal at the Home Ministry, in New Delhi's North Block, while he was working as the Deputy Director of the 'K Branch' of the Intelligence Bureau, which was on the ground floor to the right of Gate Number 7 as you entered. This was sometime in 2000. I was cutting my teeth as a journalist, reporting on New Delhi's travails in Kashmir, and I was in the North Block more often than I would care to admit. I didn't know what Jaiswal was doing there. Looking back, given the way things are today in Kashmir, I must say, neither did his colleagues, seniors and juniors. But I digress.

I caught up with Jaiswal later in the middle of 2007 in Chennai where I had become a newspaper bureaucrat. Jaiswal had been posted there some years earlier and he was soon to become Chief Minister Karunanidhi's 'Intelligence Czar', holding the rank of additional director general of police (ADGP).

The following incident happened in early 2009 and it should give the reader some insight into Jaiswal's attitude towards his profession.

Inside Hall No. 3 of the Madras High Court, 17 February 2009

Dr Subramanian Swamy, dressed in a spotless white kurta, appeared before Justices P.K. Mishra and K. Chandru to implead himself in a case to challenge the Tamil Nadu government's takover of the Nataraja temple at Chidambaram. What happened thereafter had no bearing on the Nataraja temple.

This was Tamil Nadu, where the Liberation Tigers of Tamil Eelam (LTTE) and Velupillai Prabhakaran had cast a powerful spell of magic on Tamil Nadu's politics before Prabhakaran was meted out a death you could not have wished even upon a rabid dog. During the proceedings, twenty or so advocates barged into the courtroom and hurled rotten eggs on the Harvard-educated politician. Scuffles ensued. There were reports of manhandling as well.

Given the furore the incident raised, the judges passed an order to the police to take criminal action against the perpetrators. The lawyers pleaded that they were on boycott of the court since 29 January 2009 – a boycott that included fasts and processions – all in support of the Sri Lankan Tamils; they clearly stated that they were not supporting the LTTE. Dr Swamy had demanded persistently that Velupillai Prabhakaran be deported to India to stand trial for the assassination of Prime Minister Rajiv Gandhi. The rotten eggs were mere tokenisms hurled in the name of the Tamils in Sri Lanka. The Armed Reserve Police were called in and they entered an already murky situation. A complicated Mexican stand-off developed.

A day or so later when fifteen advocates were led into the B4 police outpost in the Madras High Court premises, all hell broke loose. A police video of the events established the basic plot. At 3.45 p.m. the police arrested some lawyers and herded them inside a van. A general scrimmage began during which some lawyers ran into the court building. A couple of minutes later, stones were thrown. The lawyers had started it and the police returned the compliment, though it was clear that they were not giving as good as they were getting. (I would say 5:1 in favour of the black-coated advocates.)

By 4 p.m. stones littered the area, and there was shattered glass in the court buildings and the car park. By 4.15 p.m.

police had withdrawn to the area in front of the B4 police station, that had a sanctioned strength of over a hundred policemen (the court registrar would write to the Home Secretary on 24 February, requesting him not to post any policewomen in the court premises). The police were almost barricaded by motorcycles and scooters laying prone on the ground. At 4.42 p.m. the video footage recorded a fire breaking out on the court roof. At 5.02 the lawyers advanced throwing stones. By 5.30 the police had withdrawn well behind the B4 station, the lawyers overrunning the area vacated by the police. Obscenities flew in all directions. At 5.37 p.m. papers and chairs were set on fire, and a metal cupboard from inside the police station was dragged out and thrown into the fire. A fire engine screamed its way upon the scene but then, under the onslaught of stones, it retreated. With B4 station flaming both inside and outside, the police carried away an injured colleague. As the light faded at 5.45 in the evening, the police rushed in swinging their lathis. This marked the end of the video.

Unfortunately, no video of what happened later was available, when the lathis did all the talking. The lathis, we journalists, would report, spoke emphatically and equally to cars, motorcycles, advocates, journalists and even judges, though the last-mentioned category preferred not to advance complaints. The Supreme Court took suo moto cognizance of the happenings in the Madras High Court and asked Justice Srikrishna to look into the matter.

The Chief Justice of the Madras High Court issued

written directions to the government to suspend the additional commissioner of police (ACP) for mishandling the law and order situation. The chief minister too wanted to suspend the ACP. He called for a meeting to discuss the development.

It was at his spacious office in Fort St George that Jaiswal got the message about the incident in the evening. He went to the SP Special Branch and wrote a small paragraph in English. More or less, this is what he wrote: 'Suspension is a judicial function of the suspending authority. Which means that the suspending authority has to apply his mind on the available evidence and proof about the errors or lapses of any officer. The suspending authority cannot be directed by someone else, as it has been done, in this instance.'

The SP Special Branch translated it into Tamil. Jaiswal took both the English and Tamil versions and walked into the chief minister's office wherein hung a giant likeness of Thiruvalluvar, the poet saint of Tamil Nadu. The chief secretary, the home secretary, the DGP were all there, all inclined towards his suspension.

Jaiswal, after going around the enormous desk behind which Karunanidhi sat, his dark glasses shielding his inscrutable silence, handed over the Tamil version to the chief minister. The DGP read the English version and passed it around. ADGP Jaiswal sat, isolated, in one of the chairs that faced the chief minister. In the debate that followed, Jaiswal pointed out that no enquiry had been initiated against the additional commissioner, neither by the state government nor by the police. The Supreme Court had appointed the Srikrishna Commission to look into the incidents at the Madras High Court, and the report was being awaited. Hence there was no basis for suspension.

A question curled in the air – 'Wouldn't it be tantamount to contempt of court?'

'We could tell the court we are in receipt of your communication and we are looking into it,' Jaiswal responded. The chief minister agreed.

This is the eternal dilemma of Indian police officers: Will they get the necessary political backing for their actions? This situation arises because they are carefully nurtured in a culture where they seek/require political direction for every little action they take, not knowing the kind of political connections the person against whom the action is sought might possess. The police are controlled, and interfered with, not only on day-to-day basis but from hour to hour, too.

The law envisages the police to be as independent as the judiciary. The police derive power from the law, but while exercising it, that power becomes delegative. In the army, the soldier shoots at a person because they are ordered to, and the person who gives the order becomes responsible. In theory, an inspector of police can never say they were ordered to do so; they can only say as an investigative officer this was the action they took based on what was uncovered during the investigations. Yet in practice, day in and day out, all over India, all sorts of executive oral orders are issued to the police to do this or that. This perversion of the chain of command is rampant. Leadership is the first casualty in each of these myriad everyday situations.

The stories that you read here are rooted precisely in such everyday situations. They are therefore crime stories but with a difference. These are real stories. They are not arranged in any chronological order but rather shuffled to present a slice of life in the districts that make up the larger, invisible part of India, with its hard life and harder choices, where millions seethe unseen and unheard, lost to the English-newspaper-reading people. This is a nether region where criminals are also human beings, and yes, where policemen also make mistakes, and nothing is in black and white.

In a sense, this is R.K. Narayan territory – it is a small town in South India, possessing all the life and colour of a bustling commercial centre. But instead of being seen through the eyes of sign-painters and tour guides as in Narayan's novels, it is seen through the eyes of a policeman who must engage every day with the dark side of that small town and its rural surroundings. It is Malgudi seen through a dark, distorted lens.

I wrote the first of these stories, that of Ganiammal, way back in 2009, and it appears here almost in the same form and tone. The rest I heard over a period of time, whenever I met Anoop Jaiswal, and I carried them around somewhere in my mind where they lurked furtively. When I finally sat down to give life to them on 23 June 2021, I drove to Manapakkam in Chennai every evening, where Jaiswal lives after retirement. He spent most of his time immersed in physics experiments, and we would go over the stories, one per sitting. And each sitting would end with the delicious soup Neelam Jaiswal prepared, a different soup every day. And, to my satisfaction, she even garnished some of the stories with her reminiscences of the same time.

Incidentally, it was Manoj Das, the Odia bilingual writer and Sahitya Akademi awardee, who had originally wanted to write about the incident that I recounted now in this book under the heading 'Post paid'. Das lived in Puducherry at the Sri Aurobindo Ashram, a two-and-a-half-hour drive from Chennai, and the Jaiswals had met him there, and when he heard the story, he was eager to write about it and asked for the corroborative material, which was then sent to him.

But just after six months, he passed away in April 2021. In that respect, I am thankful that fate seems to have been kinder to me. When the manuscript was all done and had a rough form and shape, we travelled, Jaiswal and I, to Tuticorin to add vividity and detail, among other things, to the stories.

Things had changed of course, in these three decades that had elapsed since Jaiswal was posted there. The roads were better, with more vehicles visible, and more pucca buildings. Everyone now used cell phones; there was electricity in almost every village of the district, but the grinding poverty was still evident in the small village of Narikinaru.

But some things had not changed. The elderly people remembered Jaiswal and those long-gone days. However, caste conflicts, crimes, and, I was told, even the moneylending continues to this day. The more things change, the more they remain the same.

The people I met provided additional details and perspectives that had escaped Jaiswal's notice, even though he has a photographic memory, for which I was thankful. Truism though it might be, I daresay each of these stories would, inevitably, have had a different ending had Anoop Jaiswal not been present in their moments of occurrence.

The stylized sketch map of the district uses the old place names as given in the narrative. It should help the reader get a sense of the locations. Some names and nicknames have been changed to protect privacy.

Mumbai, March 2022

1

The Sivalarkulam Murders

The Manjolai hills are at an elevation of about 4,500 feet, about forty kilometres south of Ambasamudram. The drive to the hills is spectacular, through flat roads with fields, towns and villages on both sids for about twenty-three kilometres. Then from Manimuthar dam, the climb to the Manjolai hills begins. For thirteen kilometres as you climb through forests filled with animals and birds, the temperature keeps falling. Then it's endless tea estates rising all around you. Here, hilltops, when you can see them, have their heads buried in the clouds. Otherwise it is all shrouded in a blanket of mist, thickening and dissolving.

The Bombay Burmah Trading Company had owned many thousand hectares of tea estates there. There was a guest house there with good hosts, and the assistant superintendent of police (ASP) of Ambasamudram, Anoop Jaiswal, went there for a weekend with his wife, Neelam, and their children. He was looking forward to playing some tennis and drinking a little beer.

The jeep he had been allotted was fitted with a wireless, but as one went up the hills the reception became quite poor. When they reached, the sun burnt orange and crimson over the hills and it promised to be a glorious evening. As the jeep came to a halt, Jaiswal was surprised to be met by a constable from the Manjolai police outpost, which was meant to oversee the tea estates. The constable told him that there had been a murder in the Alangulam area, about sixty kilometres away. That meant as the ASP, Jaiswal had to leave immediately for Alangulam. The drive was past Ambasamudram and then about twenty-two kilometres further north. He told Neelam that she and the children could stay back at the guest house and he would go on to Alangulam. Neelam responded, 'What will we do here in the hills alone?' They preferred to go home to Ambasamudram. Back down the hill they went, driving as fast as possible as darkness fell swiftly and heavily.

Hurriedly, Jaiswal dropped Neelam and the children home and called a driver to take him to Alangulam. The driver's name was Xavier. On the wireless, he heard that the murder had occurred at Sivalarkulam village and Jaiswal instructed Xavier to drive straight to the village, not stopping at the police station. Above them, as they drove, clouds amassed, heavy, low and dark grey, and suddenly it started pouring. It was as if the sky had broken over their heads.

This was 1985, when police stations did not have jeeps. The inspector would have a motorcycle and the rest would use mopeds or bicycles, or take the bus, or hail a passing vehicle to get around.

Most of the local roads were not motorable. The jeep in which Jaiswal was travelling was old. Its windshield wipers had long given way and a makeshift wiper – a single, small one – was fitted where the driver sat. It sat on top of the broken windshield, and Xavier had to lean forward when the blade moved, and peer through the thick rain while he drove. Jaiswal held tightly on to the handlebar in front of him as they juddered along the unpaved roads towards Sivalarkulam. It was a remote village and because of the downpour, there were no people on the roads. Electricity had reached only a few villages back then and Sivalarkulam was not one of them.

On the wireless, Jaiswal asked where the sub-inspector was and the reply came that he had left for Sivalarkulam.

The village, when they reached it, was deserted. A small village without electricity in the middle of nowhere. There were maybe forty or fifty huts and some semi-permanent structures, and all of them seemed empty.

There was no one. Jaiswal thought they would find a couple of constables there, but there were none. There was no sign of the sub-inspector either. He asked Xavier to blow the horn of the jeep as they drove around, making rounds of the village, past the empty dwellings, the horn sounding intermittently, as rain came down in sheets.

There was nothing on the wireless either. They went into one or two of the huts but could find no one and they ran back to the jeep drenched. Finally, Xavier found a hut where a toothless old woman sat on the mud floor, staring blankly at the rain, chewing incessantly. He asked her where the villagers had gone. For a while, she kept looking at him. She cupped her hand to her ear so she could hear better. Xavier asked her again, this time much louder. She threw up her hands in a gesture that said she didn't know. Xavier asked her whether there had been trouble in the village and this time she wordlessly pointed in the direction of a small building that stood alone further up the street.

They walked to the building, leaving the jeep – Xavier in front and Jaiswal a few steps behind.

The building was small, one room was all it was, and it had a compound wall that ran low in front of it, broken in a couple of places. A sign marked it as the Revenue Department Building. Xavier pushed the gate open and started shouting, 'Sir! Dead bodies are here, sir! Dead bodies, three of them!' Jaiswal ran into the compound and there, lying face up in the hammer-hard rain, were three men.

Lightning lit up their wounds. All had cuts on their shoulders, forearms, hands and deep gashes on their necks and heads, down to the bone. The bodies had been washed clean by the rain but blood pooled along with the rising rainwater. All the men were young and the oldest possibly was not more than thirty.

One by one, Jaiswal checked their pulse for signs of life. Nothing. A wooden chair that had seen better days lay fallen on its side in the rain by the door of the building, which was open. Jaiswal stepped inside, wiping water away from his eyes and squinting. In the darkness he could not make out much. He ran to the jeep, his shoes squelching in the rainwater to grab the torch in the glove compartment, and he ran back with it.

In its weak, fading light, a calendar flipped crazily on one wall and the wind chased a few papers around the room. The only table stood incongruously by the door, and an empty glass lay on the ground. Jaiswal went around the desk fearing there would be more bodies, but there were none. Steel almirahs lined the walls. In one corner, on a wooden stool, stood a mud pot with a tap. An open wooden window kept thudding against the frame due to the wind. The torch gave out. Jaiswal kept wiping the rainwater from his face as he surveyed the bleak scene.

So, there were three bodies with injury marks, and the village was empty. Well, nearly empty, except for a toothless old woman who wasn't telling them much; there was no sign of policemen ever having got there; and there was only static on the wireless, drowned out by the roar of the rain. There was no one Jaiswal could talk to to find out what was going on.

Who were the dead men? Why had they been killed? Would there be revenge killings? Jaiswal considered going to the police station to get backup and come back, but he did not want to abandon the bodies or leave them unguarded; what if animals got to them before they returned? What if the people who killed them came and removed the bodies in their absence? It was all very baffling.

Then Jaiswal told Xavier, 'Let's load the bodies in the jeep and take them to the police station.'

Xavier immediately objected, shaking his head emphatically. The superintedent could see the shock on Xavier's face.

'I can't carry dead bodies, sir.'

'Eh?'

'We can't be carrying dead bodies, sir. It is a bad omen.'

'What?' Jaiswal shouted.

'Sir, I will not carry the bodies.'

'Are you out of your mind? There is nobody but you and me to carry the bodies. We will have to do it together. I am willing to help you.'

'Sir, I cannot. I will not.'

Exasperated, Jaiswal asked Xavier to give him the keys to the jeep and told him to get out of his sight. This was insubordination.

'I don't need a driver like you!' he yelled. 'The police don't need a driver like you. Get out!'

He went back to the jeep and drove it to the Revenue Department Building and parked it facing the compound gate. Leaving the engine and the headlights switched on, Jaiswal opened the back door of the jeep. Then, he walked towards the compound where the bodies lay, the scene now illuminated by the jeep's headlight cutting through the rain. He lifted the nearest body, clasping his hands under its arms and dragged it to the back of the jeep so he could load it. Xavier, who had been watching from a distance, came running up to him and implored, 'Sir, stop, stop!'

'Why?'

'Let me see if I can find an egg.'

'An egg? What do you want with an egg? Have you gone mad?'

'No, sir, if we break an egg, no harm will befall us when we disturb a dead body.'

'You are crazy! He is already dead. He can do nothing now. Where are you going to find an egg? Do you think you can coax a hen to lay an egg for you in the rain now? How did you get into the police force?'

But Xavier wasn't listening. He ran into the huts one by one, then came running back excitedly saying the old woman's neighbour had a bullock cart and there was a bullock tied nearby that could be yoked to it.

'What do you want to do with the bullock cart?'

'We can take the bodies in the bullock cart, sir.'

'Who is going to drive the bullock cart? You?'

'No, sir. We will find someone,' Xavier said and ran off again.

Jaiswal was exasperated and angry. He began dragging the body towards the jeep again. It was heavier than he had expected it to be. He had never tried to drag or carry a body before. Police training somehow overlooked this aspect of the job. The lungi the dead man had been wearing, soggy with rain, became unknotted and slid off, and so Jaiswal set the body down again.

Xavier came running back, shouting above the rain, 'Sir, sir, I found the eggs.' Jaiswal turned around and saw Xavier's hands extended, holding three eggs. The ASP was flabbergasted.

'What are the other two eggs for? You want to make an omelette now?'

'No, sir. You see, one egg for one body. Three bodies, three eggs. Now we will be safe, sir, very safe, and nothing will happen to the jeep also when we put them in it.'

'Do whatever you want, but do it quickly!' Jaiswal didn't want to see nor know what Xavier did with the eggs. Somehow, they loaded the three bodies into the jeep and turned it around and left the village behind. They headed for the main road, driving towards the Alangulam police station.

When they reached, there were only two constables there. It was the only structure in the village that had an electric light. It flickered in the verandah. The bodies were taken off the jeep and laid side by side on the verandah of the police station. The rain wouldn't leave the bodies alone even in the police station, slanting in and falling on them. Seeing the bodies in the wavering light, the superintendent could discern a certain resemblance in each of their faces.

Maybe they were related.

A hurricane lamp had been lit inside the police station in case the electricity failed completely. There was a small bulb that hung above the wireless set which took power from the battery that ran the mike of the wireless. It threw a weak pool of light on the desk.

Jaiswal informed the SP on the wireless. He sent a team of armed reserve constabulary to the village to prevent the situation from escalating into a caste war and to prevent revenge killing. Orders were given to comb the area for information, to recover the weapons that were used for the killings and to catch the assailants. Seeing the police arrive in lorries with guns, the villagers continued to stay away. There was no one the police could ask about what exactly had transpired.

The inspector of the area was on leave, but because this was a grave crime, the inspector from Tenkasi, which was another twenty-five kilometres away, had to come in order to take charge of the investigation. Jaiswal asked what had happened to the sub-inspector from the Alangulam police station. He was told that the sub-inspector and a constable had gone to Sivalarkulam as soon as they heard that there had been a murder. The sub-inspector's motorcycle was not working, so they had flagged a vehicle going that way to get to the village. Once at the village, they found it deserted and in the revenue office, they found four people, all stabbed. One of them had a weak pulse but was alive. He had had his belly cut open and had been holding his entrails in his hand when the sub-inspector arrived with the constable.

The sub-inspector did the only thing he could – he commandeered a bullock cart, which the constable steered while the sub-inspector sat with the barely conscious man and took him to the nearest primary health centre (PHC) some ten kilometres away. He had just reached and called from the PHC. The injured man was still alive, but the doctor was not there and the constable had gone looking for him. The injured man said his name was Armugam Konar.

The sub-inspector had asked again, and the injured man had weakly repeated his name. This information was repeated to Jaiswal over the phone.

The name seemed familiar. Jaiswal made a call to his office in Ambasamudram and had the clerk go through the register, which listed complaints. He called back and said, 'Yes, sir. Armugam Konar has met you in the past.'

'Was it over a land dispute?' Jaiswal asked the clerk.

'Yes, sir. He had come two months ago saying he owned a piece of land but was finding it difficult to irrigate it because the neighbour kept cutting off the water that flowed through an earthen channel. The neighbour claimed the land where the water flowed was his. The old man, Armugam Konar, contested this, but since the other party was from the majority community, the Thevars, he had come to you. The matter had been referred to the inspector, sir, in Alangulam.'

Jaiswal then recalled meeting Armugam Konar. He remembered telling the inspector to refer the matter to the revenue people who kept the land records and maps with a proper measure of the area belonging to each one. That was where this story had begun. A man from the Revenue Department had gone to the disputed part and had measured the area, following which he had gone back to his single-room office in Sivalarkulam and summoned both the parties to the office.

Armugam Konar had come to the revenue office that afternoon with his three sons. The four of them had sat on the ground in the compound waiting for the other party. The other party also arrived, some nine or ten of them, and had stood in a semicircle around the four who were sitting. The revenue official then came out to the small portico of the office carrying a chair.

Then he had brought out the records and sat on the chair, placed the ledger on his knees, opened the relevant page, and faced them to address them. It appeared from the land records and the maps that the old man's claim was correct. The revenue official had started speaking in favour of Armugam Konar. The moment the revenue official began to speak, the Thevars began to rapidly confabulate among themselves.

Neither the revenue official nor Armugam Konar and his sons had come there prepared for a dispute. They didn't know what hit them when the Thevars descended upon the father and the sons with aruvals (curved machetes commonly carried by farmers) that they carried. These aruvals were usually hung from a hook in their shirt collars and hidden well with a shawl thrown over the weapons.

The three sons had died on the spot. The father, Armugam, whose belly was cut open, had slumped to one side, his eyes wide with shock. The revenue official, seeing the massacre happening before his eyes, had stood up alarmed, knocking over the chair in the process. He had then run into his office clutching his ledger and maps; he closed the door behind him and had dragged the desk to barricade himself inside. Through the window he had seen the Thevars fall upon the Konars with their aruvals. He had feared the Thevars would come after him and burn the revenue office down along with all its records. All of a sudden, the Thevars had run away. When it was all quiet again, the revenue official had peeped out and he too fled the scene, thinking everybody was dead.

It took two or three days for the story to be pieced together. The villagers had seen nothing, and when the screams drew them to the revenue office there was not a soul in sight. They saw the bodies and ran away from the village fearing a bigger maelstrom.

Armugam had a wife, two daughters-in-law, and five grandchildren. All of them ran away too, thinking they would be attacked next. They did not know that Armugam had been taken to a hospital in Tirunelveli.

For three days after his sons were killed, Armugam could not speak coherently. At the PHC, when they finally found the doctor, all he could do was give him emergency first aid and send him on with the sub-inspector to the Tirunelveli General Hospital another two hours away. There, they stitched him up and sedated him heavily with painkillers. When he came out of his sleep, all he could do was weep uncontrollably. He kept asking for his three sons.

A sub-inspector was posted to record his story the minute he could tell it coherently. If he died after telling the story, that statement would be his dying declaration and would carry weight in court. If he survived, he would become a convincing witness. The revenue official turned up the next day, when things had quietened, and it was he who named the culprits, nearly ten of them. It was only then that the details could be recorded in the First Information Report.

For two days, Jaiswal remained in Alangulam in a lodge. He sent the jeep back to Ambasamudram to bring him a change of clothes, shaving kit, toothbrush and toothpaste and whatever else Neelam could think of packing for her husband who had had to take a sudden detour.

The assailants surrendered in court, probably as advised by their lawyer since they had been identified. They were sent to jail after a couple of days in police custody.

When Armugam was discharged from the hospital he moved away from Sivalarkulam village with his wife, two daughters-in-law and his five grandchildren and started living in another village nearby. On 1 April 1986, Jaiswal received orders transferring him out of Ambasamudram. He was to take command of the 9th Battalion in Manimuthar.

Before he left, the younger daughter-in-law of Armugam came to see him in Ambasamudram. She said she had noticed her father-in-law hiding something and when she asked him, he had brushed her question away by saying it was some marundu (medicine). Then he had broken down and confessed that it was a pesticide. He had planned to mix it in the food and poison the entire family, including his wife, his daughters-in-law, his five grandchildren, and himself. He said that he could not live nor support the family any more. Everything had been ruined. The younger daughter-in-law said, 'I know that I have become all too quickly a widow and have an uncertain future, but I am not ready to die. Please do something for us.'

Jaiswal met Armugam in the village he was then living in and told him, 'It is easy enough for you to commit suicide. But your children will never forgive you. You will be responsible for letting the killers of your three sons go scot-free, even though it was within your power to see that they are punished for what they did. You are abdicating your responsibility as a father. You are the eyewitness; you know the motive; you are the living evidence against them. Your testimony has been corroborated by the revenue official and corroborated by your earlier petition. The case is watertight. If you commit suicide, who will depose in the court? Who will seek justice? You have to live long enough to take revenge for what has happened to your sons.'

'But I cannot farm there any more,' Armugam told him.

'We will give you police protection. Do not farm the land yourself; lease it out till the case is over. The women can find work – they are able-bodied, and your grandchildren can go to school.'

He agreed.

One day, a year later, Armugam came with his two grandsons to the camp office in Tuticorin. He brought along someone who was related to him. Armugam said that the Thevars had got conditional bail and were free. The relative had heard that their lawyer told the Thevars that as long as Armugam was alive, they didn't have any hope of winning their case. They would all either get death sentences or life sentences. And the latter meant many long years in jail while their life slipped away. They were desperate. If Armugam could somehow be removed from the scene, the case against them would fall away. They could then be free.

Muthuraj, the sub-inspector from Special Branch, was in the office.

Jaiswal explained the situation to him, and asked if there was any way they could get the case brought forward. Muthuraj said, 'He will be killed, there is no doubt.'

Jaiswal then came up with a solution only he was capable of. He and the sub-inspector spoke to Armugam in private, instructing him to go back to Tuticorin and bring his family to the camp office, without informing anyone where they were going. Armugam was also given some money. He was told to come back the next day along with his family. Armugam's relative was only told that they would work something out and let them know.

Muthuraj suggested the name of K.S.P.S. Kannan, the owner of a salt pan of several thousand acres. Kannan also had some farms spread over a hundred acres near Srivaikuntam. Muthuraj requested Kannan to give Armugam Konar and his family shelter in his farm in exchange for their labour. Even the Alangulam police station was not informed where they had been relocated. Armugam's land had already been sublet, and money was arranged to be deposited in the bank.

It took one and a half years for the trial to start at Tirunelveli. For one and a half years, Armugam and his family remained incommunicado, working on the farm of

Muthuraj's friend. When the trial started, Jaiswal called the SP in Tirunelveli, requesting security be provided to Armugam when he came to depose in court. This was done. The accused, all nine of them, were found guilty. Two got life sentences, and the rest were given ten years in jail.

2

The Man Who Shot Dharmarajar Dead

Jaiswal was promoted to SP from ASP and was given charge of Tirunelveli East district, which after a few months would become Tuticorin District. He had had very little experience as a subdivisional officer. Apart from administrative work, the deputy superintendent of police (DSP) does most of the fieldwork in the subdivision. Usually, the SP is in charge of a district which has four or five police subdivisions. Although Anoop had five months of experience as ASP in Ambasamudram, a small town in Tirunelveli district, his proficiency in Tamil left much to be desired.

During these five months, he was nervous as well, worried that he would do something wrong, or make a misstep that would add to the chorus that he was no good at his job. He trod carefully, and as a result, he was nice to everyone, given his lack of knowledge and confidence. This prompted many people to come and register complaints at his office, even petty complaints. If there was a minor quarrel between neighbours, they would come to him. He would call up the police station and urge the station house officer (SHO) to settle it. Police personnel laughed at some of his efforts. They joked that the ASP was attending to trivial work which should be done by head constables.

It was in such a situation that he was posted to Tirunelveli as SP.

Tirunelveli East was a very violent district. It included the subdivision of Tuticorin, which had the highest crime rate in all of Tamil Nadu. It was often called an ASP subdivision because new IPS officers would be posted there to learn on the job, considering the prevalence of violence in the district.

When Jaiswal was being briefed about the notorious characters of the region, he learnt about Dharmar, alias Dharmarajar. Three years ago, he had killed a head constable and cut his body into twelve pieces. Dharmarajar hadn't been caught and was absconding. He followed this up with an attack on a sub-inspector. He had gone after him with an aruval. Fortunately, the sub-inspector had survived, but he still carried the cut marks on his right shoulder.

Many of Dharmarajar's crimes were unreported. He lived in an area that had a profusion of mullukadu (thorny shrub jungle) and a hillock. Nobody was willing to come forward to give a clear description of this criminal. Jaiswal heard that he had the support of his scheduled caste community.

Because of his notoriety and boldness, even the dominant community made this as a cover to settle scores with others. There were many robberies in trains recorded against him.

The DGP had announced a reward for his capture. Dead or alive, they didn't care, as long as Dharmarajar was hauled in. The amount was ₹25,000, a very high sum for the time. But even for that kind of money, nobody seemed to have seen Dharmarajar.

It was a holiday, a Sunday. There was not much happening. It was eleven in the morning or so, and Jaiswal was sitting at home when his doorbell rang. A traffic policeman was ushered in with a woman. She must have been no more than fifty. The traffic policeman saluted and said, 'Sir, this woman is moving with a piece of paper searching for a vada nadu karan (a north Indian person), a police officer called "Anub Jaibal".'

Jaiswal addressed the woman in Tamil. 'Vanga Amma, Naanthan Anub Jaibal.' (Please come, I am Anub Jaibal.)

She said she was from the village of Paraipatti in the Kadambur police station limits. Her daughter was married to an army man posted in Etawah. He would come on leave to be with his wife and then he would return to wherever he was posted at the time.

At this point, the woman began to weep. She could barely compose herself to tell the story. The previous night, after dinner, her daughter had gone outside the house to answer a call of nature. On her way back home, Dharmarajar had appeared with an aruval which he had positioned around her daughter's neck, dragged her to a nearby area and raped her. Her daughter had not been able to cry out for help because the aruval was around her neck. She came back home with bleeding bruises on her neck and told her mother what had happened.

'Have you gone to the police station?' Jaiswal asked.

'Police? They will do nothing. They have done nothing so far. Already they are scared of Dharmar.'

'Who gave you my name?'

She said she had a relative who told her that in Ambasamudram there was a police officer from north India who listened to the complaints of the people and helped them. She said that she had left her daughter at home and had taken the first bus in the morning to Ambasamudram, forty kilometres away from her village. When she reached Ambasamudram, she found out that the 'vada nadu police adhikari' (the police officer from north India) was not in Ambasamudram but in Tirunelveli. So, she had taken another bus to Tirunelveli, over an hour and a half away, and a good forty kilometres east. At the bus stop, she had asked everyone where Anub Jaibal was. A traffic policeman heard her story and brought her straight to the camp office.

'Amma intha aal yenga irrukan, intha Dharmar?' (Where is this man, this Dharmar?) asked Jaiswal

'Oorla irukkan aiyyah,' replied the lady. (In the village, sir.)

'Paraipatti liya?' (In Paraipatti?)

'Ammam, aiyyah.' (Yes, sir.)

'Nalla theriyuma?' (Are you sure?)

'Ammam, aiyyah. Adikadi namba avana paapom, aiyyah. (Yes, sir. We see him often, sir.)

Jaiswal asked her to sit down and called the Special Branch inspector, who was available, and described the situation. The inspector was of the opinion that the local police would not act.

'Is there any bold officer in my district, my entire district, that I can rely on?' asked Jaiswal. 'Give me any name. One name.'

The Special Branch inspector thought for a while and said, 'The Vilathikulam inspector, Inspector Perumal, sir.'

Vilathikulam was about a hundred kilometres away. Jaiswal picked up the wireless. The wireless was on all the time, and on it he could directly communicate with any police station. There was a code. The superintendent was always Mike Ten. The DGP was Mike 1. Jaiswal spoke into the wireless with urgency, 'Mike Ten, Vilathikulam. Mike Ten, Vilathikulam. Ask Inspector Perumal to catch the next bus or taxi, or take a motorcycle, whatever is the fastest, and rush to my office. He should leave immediately and rush here. I repeat, immediately.'

'Anyone else?' Jaiswal asked the Special Branch inspector.

He said, 'Kovilpatti Sub-Inspector Marimuthu.'

Again the wireless crackled with Jaiswal's voice, 'Mike Ten, Kovilpatti, send Sub-Inspector Marimuthu to my camp office immediately. Mike Ten, Kovilpatti. Sub-Inspector Marimuthu to come to my camp office within the hour.'

Jaiswal asked the Special Branch inspector if there were more personnel they could call on. He replied that they could and from Tirunelveli itself. Jaiswal asked him for the names.

Around three in the afternoon, the inspector from Vilathikulam was in the office. The sub-inspector from Kovilpatti had reached earlier.

When Jaiswal explained the situation, Perumal was hesitant. 'Aiyyah, this is not my area.' He then glanced at Marimuthu, who was silently looking down at his shoes. As superintendent of police, Jaiswal had the authority to depute those within his jurisdiction for such assignments. But he too was new. He was weighing what he should do when the telephone rang. It was his wife, Neelam. She was calling to say that tea was ready. Jaiswal told her that he was in the middle of a very important discussion and that she should send the tea, four cups of it, to the office.

Neelam responded, 'Why? You call them all inside. I have made some bajjis and it will take five minutes to fry some more. You can have your very important discussion inside.'

At that time Jaiswal didn't know that it was rare for an SP to invite a sub-inspector or inspector to his private quarters and into his drawing room, with the SP's wife serving bajjis and tea. He didn't know what his wife had put in the tea or the bajjis, but once they were done with the refreshments, Perumal stood up and said, 'Sir, if you have my back, I'll do whatever you want me to.' Marimuthu also warmed up to the idea.

'You select the constables you want in the team,' Jaiswal told Perumal.

Perumal began rattling off the names, and they got the wireless and ordered each person to come to the camp office as quickly as possible – even if it meant they used the DSP's jeep to get there.

Afterwards, the woman from Paraipatti talked to Perumal and Marimuthu. She told them about the village and Dharmarajar. By seven, the constables who had been summoned began arriving.

Perumal and Marimuthu came up to Jaiswal and said that from the woman's description of Paraipatti and the terrain, vehicles could not be taken to Paraipatti. The sound of the vehicle would alert Dharmarajar and he would run away. The area was covered with shrub forest and hillocks.

There were no motorable roads. Marimuthu suggested another way to get to Paraipatti. Along the village ran a railway line, and the trains going to Tuticorin would go that way. If they could get into the train, they could enter the village without raising an alarm.

There was a copy of railway timings in the office. It showed that trains coming from Madras passed the Paraipatti area early in the morning. They, the police raiding party and the woman from Paraipatti, set off for the Kovilpatti railway station. Jaiswal requisitioned weapons from the armoury for the constables – pistols, revolvers and .303 rifles. The nature of the mission had not been revealed to them. The guns and ammunition had been loaded separately. They reached Kovilpatti around eleven in the night.

At the Kovilpatti railway station, before they got down to the platform, the weapons were handed out. Jaiswal met the stationmaster who said there was a train that, if it arrived on time, would pass Paraipatti around five in the morning, as the day was breaking. The stationmaster was unwilling to order the train to halt at Paraipatti for the raiding party to get off. There was no halt scheduled there. As Jaiswal wondered what could be done, Perumal said he would handle it. The others sat on the platform waiting for the train to come. When it arrived, Perumal went to talk to the engine driver as Marimuthu supervised the loading of weapons and ammunition. The engine driver agreed to slow down the train at Paraipatti just when it would get to the main hillock. That would be slow enough for the people to jump off. The engine driver agreed to take some personnel in the engine. Others got into a bogie. It was decided that they would jump off the train not on the side facing the village but on the other side.

The plan was that Jaiswal would post an armed reserve party that he had at his disposal behind a hillock, in case the area had to be cordoned off and combed, should Dharmarajar give the raiding party the slip. They were deployed accordingly.

From the station, while the raiding party proceeded to Paraipatti, Jaiswal left by road for Kadambur, fifteen kilometres from Paraipatti. It took a little over an hour, and at the Kadambur police station he waited near the wireless for information about where they could deploy. He kept looking at his watch. It must have been anxiety, but it seemed to him that the minute hand and second hand had chosen that day to stop moving. Then came a wireless message that two people had been killed. No other details were given.

Two? Did they get Dharmarajar? Was the police party safe? Jaiswal started calling Perumal on his wireless but could not get through. Then his driver came into the room to inform him that Perumal had called to say they had done the job. Jaiswal was relieved and ecstatic. He then set off for Paraipatti.

By the time he reached Paraipatti, the sun had come out and was beaming all around. So was the entire village. People were out everywhere. The raiding team and the team in charge of cordoning were standing here and there, and a great hubbub hung heavy in the air. He was told that both Dharmarajar and his brother had been killed.

'Where are the bodies?'"

'Up there, aiyyah. By the big rocks on the hillock.'

Jaiswal flashed a message to his superior, the deputy inspector general, and went to the spot. This was what he learnt there: The train had slowed to a crawl at Paraipatti station and the raiding party had jumped off the train with their weapons. The woman had also jumped off. She lost her balance and had to be helped up. But once she recovered, she led the party straight to Dharmarajar's house. However, there were two houses there and the party was confused about the one which held Dharmarajar. Hearing their approach, the neighbourhood dogs started barking. This alerted Dharmarajar who made a run for the hillock which had shrub jungle and sheltering rocks that rose barely fifty feet behind his house. His brother had also run behind him carrying a cloth bag full of country bombs.

Paraipatti was in the pattas belt or the bomb belt, where fireworks were produced for festivities, not far from Kovilpatti and Sivakasi. Everybody in the area knew how to make bombs. First, the explosive materials, ammonium nitrate, sulphur and shrapnel in the form of blades, pins, sharp-edged quartz-like stones were placed in a paper, and a thin jute rope was wrapped around the bundle. That was it. The bombs were meant to explode on impact. They were very effective to trap animals like rabbits. They were ripped apart and died instantly. Their efficacy when used against humans, however, was doubtful. Given the extraordinary levels of violence in the district, these bombs were pressed into use during caste clashes, bootlegging deals, money-lending schemes and simple acts of revenge.

Dharmarajar's brother kept throwing these bombs at the police, covering his escape as Dharmarajar had run off towards the jungle behind him. Some of the country bombs exploded, some rolled harmlessly down the hillock. Two constables caught the bomb pellets on their legs and cried out in pain and hobbled about. (Later, they showed Jaiswal their bleeding legs.) When the country bombs began exploding, the raiding party, which numbered twenty, scattered without command and control, and it was every man for himself. Neither of the criminals was in sight any longer. Only the inspector and the sub-inspector had the wireless – they had to shout at the top of their voices to communicate with the others. In the process, they must have alerted the brothers of their every movement. Everyone on the team was nervous because no one had spotted Dharmarajar yet.

One of the constables, Vijay, filled with equal amounts of trepidation and bravado, started climbing the hillock looking this way and that, his .303 rifle at the ready. He tried to skirt a big rock ahead of him to climb further, when someone put a gun to his head. Vijay felt the cold metal muzzle at the back of his head. His own rifle was pointing in the opposite direction. From the corner of his eye Vijay saw that it was a country-made gun. Then he noticed the person squeeze the trigger. There was a click that seemed very loud. Vijay knew he was going to die – he just knew it – even as he turned to face the shooter. In front of him, his assailant loomed tall. He saw the eyes of the shooter widen in surprise when the gun didn't fire, when he squeezed the trigger again. By then, Vijay, shivering with fear, pointed the barrel of the .303 directly at the attacker's jaw.

Inadvertently, Vijay pulled the trigger of his rifle. The bullet went through the jaw of the attacker, lifting him off the ground, shattering his face. The crack of the rifle had been so loud that Vijay's ears were ringing. The rifle jerked out of his hands and fell on the ground. It was then Vijay saw that he had wet himself. His assailant lay bleeding and twisted at his feet.

Hearing the shot, Dharmarajar's brother broke his cover

and was promptly shot by two constables. Dharmarajar was writhing on the ground when the others converged around him and got a few shots at him as well. Leaning against the big rock, Vijay pulled out a small cannister of water he carried in his belt and poured its content on his pants, and drank the rest of it. He was sweating profusely, even in the gentle sunshine.

The villagers climbed up the hillock like converging worker ants. The woman who had come to them seeking justice for her daughter ran up to the spot and exclaimed, 'Avanthan antha drohi, avanthan Dharmar! Avanthan athu, avanthan athu.' (This is the wrongdoer! He is Dharmarajar! He is Dharmarajar!) Only then did Vijay realize whom he had shot. Then they had concluded that the other person, the country-bomb thrower, was Dharmarajar's brother.

Jaiswal was happy, but the deputy inspector general of police (DIG) was worried. Jaiswal told him, 'Sir, there is no confusion. Here is a murder case accused who has been shot dead. He was a wanted man with a reward on his head. Yesterday, he had raped someone as well. CRPC gives us the power – when in pursuit of a person who is accused of an offence punishable by life sentence or death, police can go to the extent of causing death.'

The DIG cut him short, 'Anoop, don't talk law like this. It looks pretty on paper when you read it at the academy. Here it is real life. Now, what you have done requires diligent paperwork. It has to be properly framed which you may not be able to do. I am sending Bhoopathy immediately to supervise this. Don't do anything till he comes.'

By half past nine in the morning, DSP Bhoopathy, who was older than Jaiswal by many years, arrived at the spot. In the evening, the collector wanted to come to the spot for an enquiry. The tehsildar had already informed the village of the collector's imminent arrival. The collector was Mr Bindu Madhavan. Jaiswal had met him once, as required by protocol, when he had joined duty at Tirunelveli. The collector had earlier called Jaiswal and said he wanted to go to the village. Jaiswal said he was in Kadambur. The bodies had been brought to the police station for an inquest. Then, they had been sent for the post-mortem.

When the collector arrived at Kadambur, they drove to the village, the collector in his own car, and Jaiswal in his camp office jeep. When they reached near the village something struck Jaiswal. He informed the collector that since he was going to enquire into the police action, it would not be proper for Jaiswal to be present there. He told him that he would wait while the collector conducted his enquiry. The collector did not contradict him.

His car went ahead and Jaiswal stepped out of the jeep, waiting for him to finish his investigation. He knew it was going to take some time. In the distance, he could see a crowd that had gathered to wait. It was a big crowd. Later, he was told that even the folks from surrounding villages had come to know of Dharmarajar's death and had turned up in strength. The collector's car stopped when it could no longer proceed further because of the swarm of people. Before he could get out of the car, the crowd surged towards Jaiswal's jeep. The people had come with garlands and flowers, which they threw on the superintendent. Soon his jeep also was covered with garlands and flowers and petals. One person applied vermilion and sandalwood paste on the bonnet and windshield of the jeep; someone broke a coconut in front of the jeep and lit camphor.

That night at home, Anoop prepared a full report to be sent to the DGP, the collector and Jaffer Ali, the DIG. He went to the DIG's office the following morning to hand over the report.

'All this is fine, Anoop. But there is a problem. You know there is a by-election. This encounter will create problems. Don't you think you could have put off this encounter till after the elections? The people who belong to this man's caste will now not vote for the minister.'

Anoop was flabbergasted.

'Sir, this man had been absconding for years. The encounter should have taken place earlier. I had just got the information about his whereabouts, sir, and I lost no time in acting on it.'

The next morning, he got a call saying, 'Anoop, you have to suspend the policemen who were in the encounter party.'

Jaiswal was devastated, even though his seniors said that the suspension would be revoked soon enough after things calmed down. He couldn't believe what was being said. The experience of going to the Supreme Court had made an abiding impression on him. He did not trust what was being said orally. He discussed this with the inspectors, and then he told his wife to be prepared for another suspension. He went to his office and wrote a short letter to the authorities. 'I have been asked to suspend the police party that went to capture or kill Dharmarajar. The police party was formed under my command and acted on my direction. Hence, if anybody has to be suspended for this action, it is me and nobody else.'

And because he did not trust anyone, he marked separate copies to the DIG, the collector and the DGP.

Jaffer Ali was fond of Jaiswal. He called him and said, 'Anoop, why did you do this? This would have gone away. They would have settled the matter.'

'Sir, I don't trust anyone any more. Who can say that tomorrow they will not take back their word on the suspension. The innocent should not be hanged, sir. I suffered for two years, and you know it.'

With the threat of suspension hanging over their heads, the raid party lay low. They did not utter a word about the encounter. Then word got around that Jaiswal had himself killed Dharmarajar. No one listened to Jaiswal's protestations that he had been nowhere in the vicinity when the encounter had occurred.

Despite these proceedings, celebrations were in full swing all over the Gurumalai panchayat area to which Paraipatti belonged. It was like Pongal had come early. Evidently, many more had suffered at the hands of Dharmarajar than the police had records of. Dharmarajar's sister was also arrested.

Subsequently, Jaiswal came to know that she was known as Kovilpatti Veeralakshmi, alias Kutti Phoolan Devi. She was a bigger terror than her brother and had assisted her brother in his criminal activities. It was she who had cut the head constable into twelve pieces, not Dharmarajar. The head constable had raised his hand at Dharmarajar's sister over some crime she had committed. Dharmarajar had murdered the constable for that. His sister had then insisted he be cut into pieces and she did it herself. That was what was said. The newspapers went to town with the story. 'Kutti Phoolan Devi Arrested' said one banner headline.

The other big story was that of the relief in the village, the celebrations. Seeing the mood, it was decided that the move to suspend the policemen who were part of the raid party that had killed Dharmarajar be dropped. The enquiry was conducted at the Kovilpatti taluka office by the deputy collector. Witnesses were examined, and the report was filed a month later. The enquiry upheld what had transpired.

A month later, Anoop was again at the Kadambur police station on a routine inspection visit. As he approached the police station, he saw crowds on both sides of the road. As the jeep entered the compound of the police station – and the Kadambur police station had a big compound – he saw it was filled with men, women and children. They were attired in their finest. Jaiswal was slightly alarmed. He thought the officials at Kadambur had failed to inform him that there was a situation at the police station. But there stood in front of him the inspector and the sub-inspector. They were grinning from ear to ear.

'What is the problem?' he asked.

'No problem, sir. No problem at all,' the inspector replied after he had saluted.

'What is all this crowd for then?'

'They are here to see the person who shot dead Dharmarajar.'

'You know, baba, more than anybody else, that I have not done that. I was not even at the spot. You know that!'

'Try telling them that, sir. Try telling them!'

As Superintendent Jaiswal stepped out of the jeep, they continued to smile. It was getting a bit embarrassing.

3

Fish Curry and Rice

Anoop Jaiswal, IPS, and Tuticorin's new SP, was to travel in the morning to Tirunelveli to meet the DIG. It was around an hour's drive.

He started from his home in the suburbs, in State Bank Colony, which was also his camp office, and was on his way. Ten minutes later, when he had travelled four or five kilometres, he remembered he had to make an important telephone call. Jaiswal asked the driver if there was any police station nearby and he replied, 'Sir, Tuticorin South Police Station is very nearby.'

It was around seven-thirty in the morning. The moment the superintendent's white ambassador car with its red revolving light stopped outside Tuticorin South police station, there was a slight commotion inside. People began cleaning up and constables started to run around. In 1987, Tuticorin district had thirty-nine police stations. Even as he walked into the room of the SHO, an inspector stood up and saluted him. When Jaiswal sat down to make the call, he could hear somebody shouting from the lockup. The shouting was continuous and loud; he asked the SHO what the matter was and who was the person making a ruckus in the lockup.

'Sir, he is a rowdy, sir. Very bad fellow. We have just arrested him,' the SHO said.

'What for?' asked Jaiswal

He said the rowdy had barged into the police station and had abused the police.

The new superintendent was surprised. For a ruffian to come to the police station alone and abuse the police officers required massive courage.

'Call him here,' he instructed the SHO. 'What is the problem?'

The SHO said, 'No, sir. Don't call him. He is in a very bad mood and has a foul mouth. He will use bad words against you. He is an HO, sir.' (HO was the short form for Habitual Offender.)

'Doesn't matter. Call him,' the new superintendent persisted.

They brought Antony Mookkan before him – a short, lean man wearing spectacles. He appeared to be in his mid-fifties, guessed Jaiswal.

Antony wore a lungi and a shirt. He had grey stubble on his chin. He stood with his hands folded in front of him, and the SP could see his hands were swollen. A habitual offender is someone who has many cases pending against him, sometimes thirty or forty, and he or she is in and out of jail all the time for burglary, theft, pickpocketing, cases of liquor and drug peddling – small cases and petty crimes.

'What happened?' Jaiswal asked the inspector.

Before the inspector could reply, Antony said in Tamil, 'Ni than SP ya?' (Are you the SP?) 'Ni' is less respectful than 'Ningal', which is used to address elders or strangers.

The SP's Tamil, though poor, was good enough to pick up that.

'I am the SP. What is the issue? Why are you shouting and abusing the police?'

'Ithu thaan unn nyayam a? Naan thappu panna, nee yennakku thaan adi kodukanam, nee yennai thaan arrest pannanum. Yennodiya manaiviyai yethukkaaga thontharavu pannarai?' (Is this your justice? If I am at fault, you should arrest me and beat me. Why did you mistreat my wife?)

'What is the matter?' the SP asked the inspector.

It was the practice of the police to check on habitual offenders in the police station limits in the night, to keep tabs on them and to remind them that the police were alert and watching, and that they should not get up to any mischief. If the offender was not at home when the police arrived for the checks, they were to have a proper alibi for not being in the house at that time of the night. Sometimes, the police would wait for the offender to come home, or someone in the house would tell them where the person in question was.

The police had gone to Antony's house at two or three

in the morning, but nobody had responded. It was an old door and when they had pushed hard, it had given way. They entered to find a lamp burning and a woman sleeping on the floor. The police then asked her to get up, but she refused. They asked her again and still she didn't do as they said. So, irritated and exasperated, one of the policemen, a constable, kicked her to make her move.

The woman howled and shrieked and said Antony was not there and that she did not know where he had gone. She added that the police could ask him themselves when he returned and that they ought to leave her alone.

When the police kicked Antony's wife, it caused the wound swollen with puss and blood to rupture and stain her saree. She developed a septic wound around her knee. It became so swollen that her entire body started to swell up. For three to four days, she was wracked by a raging fever, and in her delirium she became convinced that she was knocking on death's door. Seeing her restless, drifting in and out of sleep, covered in sweat, Antony also thought that she was going to die. He was prepared for it. After the police incident, she rebuked Antony, 'Because of your activities, I can't even die in peace. What a fate you have brought upon me, Antony!'

In a rage, Antony had left his wife to continue her journey out of this world alone and had barged into the police station to hurl abuses at the policemen. They had caught him and put him in the lockup.

Antony requested, 'Let me go for two days. Two days

only. Once my wife is gone, I will return and surrender and you can foist all the cases you want against me. But for now, because my wife is dying, I want to be by her side. I have to be by her side.'

'But you left her and came to the police station yourself.'

'I was angry that they had kicked her. I am still angry that they kicked her. What did they do that for? They could have come back and arrested me, anyway. They don't need a reason to do that – they are the police.'

'You are under arrest, so I can't let you go, but I will not let your wife die like this,' Jaiswal said.

His friend, Dr Ravindran, ran a nursing home called Rajam Clinic on WGC Road, near the bus stand. He called him from the station phone and explained the wife's situation to him. Jaiswal asked him if he could send an ambulance to collect her and treat her at his clinic. Dr Ravindran agreed to it, and Jaiswal informed the inspector that he was proceeding to Tirunelveli and that the inspector should oversee the care of Antony's wife.

Later, he learnt that Antony was briefly remanded on a petty case he was wanted for, and his wife had been operated upon successfully. She had had an ulcer and the pus had gathered inside the wound. They drained it out, cleaned it and closed the wound so that it could heal. For fifteen days, she was admitted in Rajam Clinic. Then, she was discharged.

Late one night, more than a month or two later, Antony brought his wife to the camp office.

The State Bank of India Colony was in the suburbs on the

road leading to Kovilpatti. Jaiswal's office was a small room attached to his residence, which had two bedrooms and a hall, some 1,600 square feet in total. The floors were made of slippery granite. There was a guardroom, with four beds for the constables, where an armed constable was present at all times. A small garden was in the front, and at the back of the house, a nellikkai maram (gooseberry tree) showered succulent gooseberries.

It was a new colony. Most of the surrounding plots stood empty. Nearby was a small Ganesha temple. Superintendent Jaiswal and his family were the first occupants of the house. They lived on the ground floor. On the first floor, which could be accessed by a staircase from the outside, was a small room where the camp clerk sat and maintained the office records and a hall where the Special Branch had its office and a small terrace where sometimes Jaiswal flew kites with his children.

There was a calling bell outside, on the compound wall, for those who wanted to see the SP and alert the camp office. Anybody could come and see him. He received visitors up to eleven in the night and tried to meet everyone who came to see him. When he couldn't do so – which was unusual and happened only when it wasn't an emergency case – he provided dhurries (heavy cotton rugs) to the callers to spend the night at the bus stand nearby, which had a sheltering roof and a bench. They were then told that the SP would see them in the morning after seven. These people would spread the dhurries on the cement floor and sleep on them.

The SP usually had many visitors, with all kinds of problems and requests, and they came from the surrounding villages and areas as well.

Outside by the garden, there was a room which was not connected to the house and was used as his office. It was a small room; at the most it was ten feet by ten feet of floor space. There was a large desk and an almirah. It had two windows, one in the back and one on the side. The side window was kept open. There was a wireless that was always on, although Jaiswal could turn the volume down when he needed to. There were two wooden chairs for visitors to sit, although most who came to see him remained standing.

On that day, Antony had come to thank him. He had taken to visiting Jaiswal from then on. Jaiswal would call him in last, after he had seen the other visitors, and Antony would be waiting. When he came in, he would sit on the floor. He would give petty information about both criminals and the activities of the police. Many of his tipoffs were denied by the superintendent's colleagues; some were exaggerations and some false, but many turned out to be right. In policing, obtaining reliable information is an art that requires discernment.

Sometimes, Antony gave information pertinent to the customs department. Tuticorin had a big port and was infamous for smuggling. One night, while Antony was talking to Jaiswal, a man and his wife were ushered in. They were agitated. It was around 8.30 or 9 p.m. The man said they had been waylaid and robbed. It had happened on a bridge on the outskirts of the town. A log had been laying across the road preventing his scooter from going further. When the man had dismounted from his scooter to move the log out of the way, two people armed with sticks, aruvals and sickles robbed them of their purse, watch and thali (mangalsutra).

Jaiswal said, 'Why have you come here? Please go and register a case in the Town South Police Station immediately.' He called the police station and found that two other people were sitting in that police station with similar complaints. After the couple had left for the police station, Antony, who had been listening, asked where the incidents had occurred and the name of the bridge. Jaiswal told him.

Antony said, 'Sir, oru vandi kudungo, anga naan odanne poi, kanndu pidichutu, naan solarein ongalukku.' (Sir, give me a vehicle. I will go there immediately and find out for you what had happened.) Jaiswal called the driver, put the camp office jeep at Antony's disposal and went to eat dinner.

Antony was back after about an hour. Jaiswal asked the driver where they had gone and the driver said, 'I am not really sure, sir. We parked somewhere, and he asked me to wait. He went on foot alone, and came back a little later. Avaru yengayo poittar, saar' (He just left for some place, sir), the driver said.

Antony interrupted and said, 'Sir, the robbers are all ganja addicts. There are three of them, and they are all sleeping it off in the hut. You can send in your police and arrest them.'

He gave the location of the hut and even drew a map.

Jaiswal instructed the driver to take Antony there. But he added that the jeep should be parked somewhere in the vicinity of the hut, once Antony had pointed it out, but away from the policemen who would be rushing there to arrest the culprits. Jaiswal said, 'Let him sit hidden in the back of the jeep covered with a cloth, and don't allow the police to come near the jeep. They should not to know where the information came from.'

Jaiswal got on the wireless and sent policemen to the location to arrest the culprits. Three persons were arrested, and all the stolen items were recovered from the hut.

Sometimes, Antony would come with his wife, who was a few years younger to him. She was lean and agile and stood upright. She didn't speak much. Sometimes, she added to Antony's information or said something that led in the contradictory direction. Antony would keep quiet or nod his assent.

Occasionally, Antony was paid for his information. Jaiswal gave him money from the SR funds – the secret reward funds for the entire district of Tuticorin. It was the discretionary fund of the director general of police. He allotted it from time to time to meet payments to informants, expenses incurred during investigations and intelligence collection.

There was a lot of police work which cannot be accounted for in terms of money. Many times, the payment was for information, which when checked out yielded nothing.

Jaiswal drew the money and kept it in small amounts in separate envelopes. There would always be a thousand rupees in total, that he kept in his camp office. There was no receipt taken. Depending on the type of information, he gave out the money – sometimes even for compassionate help, such as when a visitor did not have money for the bus fare back to his village or house. Sometimes, Jaiswal gave Antony a hundred rupees, sometimes a little more.

Often, Antony would refuse the money. But if his wife was with him, and he happened to have hesitated, she would give him a nudge with her sharp elbow and he would accept the money.

One day, he came alone. The superintendent asked him in jest if he always sought permission from his wife. No, no, no, Antony protested unconvincingly, while also smiling in acknowledgement.

'Antony, tell me, you have been a murderer and you are not afraid of anybody. Why are you so scared of your wife? I often see that you don't confront her about anything; you don't even contradict her.' Antony laughed it away and then, in all seriousness, he said, 'I am not afraid. But remember, sir, I went to jail as a young man, when I was I think twenty-seven and my wife was twenty-four. She is three or four years younger than me. I got a life sentence for what I did. Don't go by what my wife looks like now. She is old now, halfway to being a hundred. She was very beautiful when she was young. Many people were after her. When I was in jail, those young men would have approached her with ulterior motives. They would have said, "Antony is going to be in jail for a long time and you are wasting your life waiting for him. He is going to be in jail for twenty years and when he comes out, you don't know how he will be." Jail changes people until you can no longer recognize them. Fifteen years I was in jail, sir, fifteen long years. When I came out of Madras Central Prison, I never expected it, but she was still waiting for me.'

Antony's voice cracked with emotion when he said that.

'She waited for me. It was as if she was serving a jail term along with me in the open, as life bustled past her. When such is the case, where is the choice for me but to be afraid of her? Our son was born a year after I came out of prison, sir. Our son.'

Jaiswal did not respond. He didn't know how to, but the next time Antony's wife came with him, the superintendent began to see her, behind the dirty, bedraggled saris she wore, as a different woman.

For many years after that, Jaiswal saw Antony, sporadically. Whenever he asked the police 'What news of Antony Mookkan?', the response was that he had gone quiet and there were no new cases against him.

Once, Jaiswal asked the chief manager of the State Bank of India (SBI), 'Why don't you finance Antony Mookkan, a fisherman who had turned into a criminal due to unfortunate circumstances? Can you give him a net and a boat and set him on a different course?'

The chief manager smiled quizzically. 'Will he repay the loan, considering his criminal record? And who will stand guarantee?'

'You work out some innovative scheme, and we will see what happens.'

Sometime later, the SBI people arranged for the financing and in the programme announcing it, Antony was brought on the stage and SBI took the credit for financing a criminal, a convicted murderer.

That evening after the function was over, the manager invited Jaiswal to a dinner at his home. There, he told the SP that he was not going to ask Antony to pay back the loan. Jaiswal asked, 'But why?'

'If you call someone to generate advertisement for you, to get him on the stage and speak about his bad past and he allows you to do that for the publicity of the bank, don't you think he deserves some concession for that?'

After that, a year passed before Jaiswal saw Antony. During that time, nobody disturbed him; even the police were scared of Antony because they knew he knew the SP and believed he would speak against them.

One time Jaiswal had gone for a month-long leave to Gorakhpur to see his parents. He returned home in the middle of the month. There was a cumbersome process by which Jaiswal had to obtain his salary slip from the office of the accountant general (AG) in Madras. His camp clerk, Velayudham, had to follow it up with the AG's office and only after that would they send the salary. Both Jaiswal and Velayudham had forgotten about it and when the first of the month came, Jaiswal realized he had not received the salary because the AG's slip had not arrived. In those days, an SP's salary was three thousand rupees. Jaiswal chided Velayudham about it, 'Look Velayudham, you forgot about my salary slip, and so did I. Now there is not going to be salary for this month and my family is going to starve.'

Antony had been standing outside the camp office when Jaiswal said this. After everybody left, he came in. Antony asked Jaiswal how he was and then he smiled and said, 'I heard you are in need of money.'

'So, Antony, why are you so bothered about it?'

'Illai, ayya. oru vazhi irrukku ongalukku neriya kaas varum.' (There is a way for you to make a lot of money.)

'Except for dacoity, robbery or theft, can you tell me any other way to make money?'

'You know David?'

'I've heard of him, yes. That smuggler?'

'Yes. David's younger brother came and met me. In the olden days, I used to do some landings for them. Their ships would be in anchorage outside, and in the night, I would go out there with a boat. They would lower the goods onto the boat, and I would bring them to the shore where they were wanted. It earned me good money. Two days ago, David's brother came and told me that silver is being shipped, in large quantity, and he wanted me to bring it to the shores. I told him I wouldn't do it. He asked me to think about it and come back. He told me, "Don't say, no."

'Why? Did you say no?'

'Aiyyah, neenga yennode kai kattitinga.' (You have tied my hands.)

'No such thing. Who is stopping you?'

'Illai, aiyyah.' (No, sir.) Now, I will go and agree to do the job, and I will tell you where I am going to land with the silver. You come and seize everything. Officially, ten per cent of it will be yours. You will get more than your salary.'

'But what will happen to you? Won't they kill you?'

'Aiyyah, God is there. He will look after me. He has looked after me till now, even after I became a murderer. Aiyyah, I need my freedom. Please free me!'

The superintendent of police smiled and said, 'But Antony, I am not going to set you free.'

About a year or so later, Jaiswal was transferred to Tirunelveli but before that happened, he had introduced Antony to the customs department. One of the collectors of customs in Madurai became a friend of Jaiswal after he joined the scuba diving club that the superintendent had started. Jaiswal introduced Antony to him and told him, 'Handle Antony with care. He is a very intelligent man and can give you good information.'

Later Jaiswal learnt Antony had worked for customs for some time, but had begun to trick them. Before Jaiswal left for Madras for his deputation to the Intelligence Bureau, Antony came to meet him. Jaiswal confronted him. 'Dei, I heard you are duping the customs department.'

Antony shook his head and explained it this way, 'For five hundred rupees, they want information worth five lakh rupees. Am I a fool to give such information? They should give me a proper share, shouldn't they?'

Six or seven years later, Jaiswal had come to Madras from Delhi for some work, and his friends in Tuticorin wanted him to spend a few days there. He agreed and informed his friend K.S.P.S. Kannan and some police officers who had worked with him that he was coming, including Inspector Elluvan who been with him in Special Branch.

Jaiswal took the Pearl City Express from Madras to Tuticorin. It was a train that left from Egmore station in Madras at half past six in the evening and arrived in Tuticorin, some six hundred and fifty kilometres away, fourteen hours later, at 8.30 a.m. the next morning. He had a lower berth in the AC two-tier compartment. He read a book, lay on his berth and fell asleep. He woke up in the morning just as the train was pulling out of Kovilpatti. Tuticorin was only a couple of hours away.

Then, to his utter surprise, Antony and his wife were there, standing in the compartment.

They had been waiting for him to wake up. 'Aiyyah,' Antony said, 'I heard from the police that you were coming in this train and we came to meet you.'

Before Jaiswal could ask or say anything, they literally pushed the other passengers to the side. His wife opened a small tiffin carrier. The smell of idli and fish curry filled the AC compartment. They offered the food to him.

Jaiswal said, 'I have just woken up and I haven't even brushed my teeth. You leave it here and I will eat it later.'

His wife, though, would not listen. She ordered, 'You can brush your teeth after eating.'

Jaiswal was still reeling from the suddenness of it all. 'What are you doing in Kovilpatti? You live in Tuticorin!'

Neither of them replied to that, and they waited till he finished eating. And then, they kept talking, and Jaiswal hardly realized when Antony's wife packed up the tiffin and put it away. The train was about to stop at Maniyachchi station, less than thirty kilometres from Tuticorin. It was a short halt, for less than a minute. Jaiswal excused himself to wash his hands and brush his teeth. When he returned, the smell of fish curry was lingering in the air, but Antony and his wife were no longer to be seen.

At Tuticorin, his friends were there to receive him; among them were many police officers, including Inspector Elluvan. As he was getting into the car, Elluvan quietly asked, 'Sir, have you seen Antony recently?'

'Why? What has happened?' Jaiswal asked him.

'He is wanted in some cases, serious cases, and he is absconding for some time. When I heard that you were coming, I felt he would come and see you. I have posted some people all around, including inside the railway station, but so far we have not spotted him. Will you let us know, sir, if he attempts to get in touch with you?'

Jaiswal laughed and said, 'Your guess was not far off. But he got into the train at Kovilpatti.'

In 2001, Jaiswal had another chance to go to Tuticorin, now Thoothukudi, on an official visit. He stayed at Sagar Sadan, a secluded guest house maintained by Southern Petrochemical Industries Corporation Ltd (SPIC), about a couple of kilometres out of the town from the harbour. A long narrow road with mango trees on one side and electric poles on the other led to the guest house. The guest house was a two-storeyed curved building on a sprawling campus, behind which stood a wall of coconut trees, and beyond those were the wide beaches and the gleaming sea. Tall ashoka trees lined the boundary of the property.

There was no public transport in the area in those days. His room was large and comfortable. The mosaic flooring was cool on the hot day because both the air conditioners had been running for some time. There was one in the bedroom and one in the drawing room in the suite that he had been given. Towards noon, Jaiswal was resting when the room bell rang. The watchman sent word that there was a coolie woman waiting for him outside the gate and that she wouldn't go away. They had not allowed her in, but she had refused to leave the place. She had been waiting for nearly three hours.

The walk to the gate was through a gravel track that ended where the shaded portico began. Once out of the shade of the portico, it was a bit of a walk to the gate, and when Jaiswal reached there, he had already begun to sweat under the hot sun. He saw someone waving at him from outside the gate. It was Antony's wife.

Jaiswal asked how she and her husband were.

'Aiyyah, he is no more.'

Jaiswal remained silent. He did not have the courage to ask how it had happened. She said their son had grown up.

He was working somewhere now. She then brought out a small tiffin box. Jaiswal said he'd take it to the guest house and have it returned. She replied, 'No! You will throw it away. Please eat it right here.'

She sat on the kerb which ran beside a culvert and indicated that Jaiswal should sit down too. She produced a bottle of water as well. Over the cement culvert, Jaiswal washed his hands using a little water from the bottle, and sat down on the kerb beside her to eat the rice and fish curry. It was nethili (sardine). He ate in silence, thinking about Antony.

On that long, tree-lined empty road that ran to the harbour, with the sun blazing above them, Antony's wife watched with satisfaction as Jaiswal ate every last morsel of the food, as though it was the last meal he was going to eat. All through the meal, she did not utter a single word. Then she packed the small tiffin box and got up to leave. He didn't say anything as she walked away. He stood watching her with folded hands. After her figure receded down the road, he thought perhaps he should have organized a ride in a police jeep for her back to Tuticorin. But that afternoon, he couldn't bring himself to do anything.

That was the last time Anoop Jaiswal saw Antony Mookkan's wife. Some years later, news filtered to him that Antony's son had died in an accident. But his grandchildren were alive.

What of the murder Antony was convicted and jailed for when he was younger? The details were vague. It had happened in the seventies. Antony was in Madras working as a cook-cum-home assistant for some middle-level actress. He must have been in his mid-twenties. He doted on his mistress.

Over months, Antony found that whenever his mistress entertained a particular man, she would become tense, and sometimes she would even cry. The man was either a director or a producer. The routine would be the same. The producer would come, and afterwards they would retire to a room and shut the door behind them. After the man would leave, she would be in tears. After this scene had repeated many times, Antony plucked up the courage to ask her what the matter was. Blackmail, she had answered. She didn't want to do what the producer wanted her to do, but she didn't have a choice. She didn't know how to say no, and she didn't want to be with him either.

When she next asked Antony to cook a meal for the producer after one of his visits, Antony made some fish curry with vanjram (seer fish) and rice to go with it. For snacking with drinks, he fried some prawns. The producer liked Old Monk rum, and a bottle was kept ready. When the producer had drunk about three quarters of the bottle, and pronounced the fish curry the tastiest in the world, he was having trouble walking straight. Antony told his mistress to go to her room, lock the door and to not come out. He told her he would see to it that the producer left in a taxi without bothering her.

Seeing the producer unsteady and swaying and slurring,

she went into her room and locked it from inside. Antony led the producer to the bathroom and helped him vomit into the washbasin; he opened the tap so that he could wash his face and gave him a towel to dry his face. Then slowly and firmly, he pushed him to the bathroom floor and, straddling him with his legs, Antony held the producer's head and slit his throat with the same carving knife that he had used to cut the fish. As the producer struggled, Antony held him down and let him bleed into the closet. Finally, the producer stopped struggling. Then, Antony severed the producer's head, and then the body in two parts, stuffed them into a gunnysack, and took them out of the house. Antony had not thought through the whole crime, and the police were soon on to him and he confessed.

He had told the court it was his decision alone; his mistress had played no part in it. She had no knowledge of it and was wholly innocent. He had said he did it because he could not bear to see the tears of his mistress, who had been very kind to him.

4

Tincture Ginger Berry or How Thoothukudi Got Its Name Back

Tuticorin is called Thoothukudi in Tamil. Kudi can mean two things, a settlement or a drink. Both apply to the town of Thoothukudi. It has large settlements around the two harbours, the fishing harbour and the main harbour. And daily wage earners and fishermen would drink copious amounts of something called tincture ginger berry. It sounds exotic, like something you could sip in an upscale bar, but in reality it was illicit liquor, with a very high alcohol content.

Vodka, if you drink it neat, as the Russians do, is often forty-one per cent proof. Tincture ginger berry had eight-six per cent proof, sometimes higher. They called it inji, which in Tamil means ginger. But really, ginger was just a minor ingredient, which was used to suffuse nearly hundred per cent proof alcohol, which is why it was a tincture.

Jocularly, Thoothukudi was called Injikudi because of this drink. In the early and mid-eighties, it was sold in medical shops, although it is difficult to determine what medicinal purpose it served exactly. But it was readily available over the counter.

In many medical shops, a glass cup was kept in one corner of the counter and whenever people who lined up behind it asked for inji, money changed hands and a shot was poured into the cup. It would be gulped down and the customer would step away and make way for the next one. By the time the person who had had it walked a few steps, the alcohol would hit him. It was not a polite drink that worked its way gently into your bloodstream. The mechanics of the drink was chaotic. The superintendent of police, Jaiswal, was told that when you drank it your throat burned and all too soon you felt groggy and high, before you could take a few steps.

The sale was done openly. There was nothing covert about it. The public bought it, drank it and got high. There was political support for it, otherwise it wouldn't have been sold so openly. Tuticorin was the hub for the sales. How and from where it was brought to Tuticorin, nobody knew.

Superintendent Jaiswal called for records that the police had on it. That was when it was discovered that there were no records or statistics of what had been done to check the issue. If there were no records with the police, and it was going on all around openly, it was a good bet that money was being paid to the police.

In 1986, Jaiswal convened his first crime meeting as the

superintendent of the recently formed district of Tuticorin. This was a meeting where the superintendent set the overall directives, objectives, tasks and trajectory for the month.

Jaiswal instructed everyone that he did not want this liquor to be sold anywhere in the district any more. They listened politely. There was a murmur behind his back: 'This new SP has come with a small blade. And he wants to cut down a giant tree with it!'

The sale of inji continued unhindered. One evening Jaiswal wore a kurta pyjama, got into the camp office jeep, asked Kanakaraj, the driver, to sit beside him and drove to the WGC Road. The road ran perpendicular to the waterfront and led to the main harbour. It was a wide road, the equivalent of Mount Road in Madras, that runs from Fort St George to St Thomas Mount. The biggest shops of Tuticorin squatted all along this wide, arterial street.

Jaiswal parked the jeep by the side of the road, instructed the driver to remain there and he walked down the road, carrying a small leather bag. All around him the Tuticorin evening turned a deep crimson as darkness fell. Further down the road, he saw a small crowd thronging a corner of a medical shop. People were paying for a brown liquid that was being poured into a cup and, one by one, those who paid were gulping it down and going away. It was all very orderly and smooth.

Jaiswal went near the shop and asked someone who was walking back from it, 'Inji yenge irrukku?' (Where could I get inji?) The man pointed to the crowd and asked Jaiswal to get in line and wait for his turn. The counter ran wide and all the way across the front of the medical shop. Jaiswal went to the part of the counter where there were no customers and saw that the same cup was being used again and again.

The transactions were quick, methodical, almost wordless. Most people brought the exact amount that was to be paid and when money changed hands the drink was poured into the cup and down the throat went the drink. The man would make a face as it went down, sometimes wipe his mouth, hitch up his lungi, and go away looking satisfied, and sometimes, only sometimes, he paid for another shot before he drank it and staggered away. Between the drinks, the cup was never washed.

Legend had it that tincture ginger berry went to work the minute it entered the mouth and got to the oesophagus and by the time it entered the stomach, the work of the alcohol was nearly done. Jaiswal didn't see anybody who wanted to buy a full bottle. There was no need, really. He would be sprawled flat out on the road or the pavement if he attempted to drink a whole bottle.

Finally, the man pouring the tincture ginger berry noticed Jaiswal standing and gestured with his hands, without a word, asking, 'What do you want?' Jaiswal uttered the word. In-ji. Jaiswal had no police to assist him, and with the crowd increasing in size, he was nervous.

The man asked, 'Yevalo venam?' (How much do you want?)

'Yellam,' Jaiswal replied. (The whole lot.)

'Yellam?'

'Yes. All. All that you have in the shop.'

The man was surprised and suspicious and asked with an undertone of threat, 'Kindala pannarai? (Is this a joke?)

Jaiswal opened the bag he was carrying and pulled out a 9mm pistol. He placed it on the counter so all could see it. Then he responded, 'Ithu unakku kindal mathiri theriyutha?' (Does this look like a joke to you?)

The man behind the counter immediately shouted to the shopkeeper who had been sitting in the anteroom behind a small desk, and everybody at the counter scrambled away and watched from a distance. Seeing the commotion, more people started arriving at the shop.

Jaiswal introduced himself. 'Naandan puthu SP, Anoop Jaiswal.' (I am Anoop Jaiswal, your new SP.) 'How many bottles do you have?'

The man pointed behind him. There were dozens of bottles. The ones that had been emptied were lying in a heap on the floor. Jaiswal directed him to place all the bottles on the counter. There were about thirty bottles. All of them were the size of a quarter bottle of rum or whisky. The bottles had no labels. He instructed that all the bottles be placed in a cardboard carton and that the salesman should carry the carton and walk with Jaiswal.

With the carton on his head, the man who sold the tincture ginger berry walked behind the new superintendent to the Central Police Station that was about five hundred yards away, the crowd following them. The sentry there didn't recognize the superintendent and Jaiswal had to tell him who he was. He entered the police station and went straight to the SHO's room.

He asked that the carton with the bottles be placed on the table of the SHO. The SHO had been sitting, but now, he stood up immediately and saluted Jaiswal. A constable cleared the table quickly and placed the carton with the bottles on it. Jaiswal told the SHO, 'We will be good friends as long as we don't find this thing again in your jurisdiction. As long as I am the SP, I don't want this happening again. Is that clear?'

Jaiswal walked back to his jeep.

The following morning the sub-inspector of the Central Police Station came to his office along with the inspector and the DSP. The DSP was an elderly person, Mr Austin, who had been promoted from sub-inspector. They were apologetic.

'There is no point in apologizing to me. I don't want this inji to be found anywhere in this district, and I am not going to repeat it,' Jaiswal told them. Soon Jaiswal learnt that in the main market, tincture ginger berry was no longer being sold, but it was still available in the outskirts.

The kingpin, he learnt, was one Balamurugan, who had two brothers assisting him. But there were also rumours that one of the brothers had fallen out with his siblings. Jaiswal pressured Austin to unearth more details.

One evening, the Central Police Station sub-inspector called him on the phone and told him that a car had been intercepted with three hundred to four hundred bottles of inji in the boot. Balamurugan's estranged brother was in it, along with the driver. Jaiswal asked that he be brought to the camp office. He wanted to know where the bottles had come from. At first Balamurugan's brother denied it, saying that he had no idea where or how they came to be in his car. The driver wouldn't reveal anything either. Jaiswal ordered that a case be registered and both be remanded.

The brother requested to speak to Jaiswal, privately. Jaiswal told him he was not interested in a bribe. That would only get him into more trouble. The brother said he didn't want to bribe Jaiswal, who then asked everyone but the inspector, Gopalakrishnan, to leave the room. The brother said, 'I beg you to spare me. Don't arrest me today.'

'Why not?'

'Sir, my wife had a heart attack yesterday.'

'You expect me to believe that a man runs around the countryside in a car full of illicit liquor while his wife has suffered a heart attack?'

'No, sir, if she hears that I have been arrested, the news will surely kill her.' He knelt on the ground and said, 'Sir, you can arrest me after five or ten days. I will come and surrender. You can keep the car and the bottles with you, but please don't arrest me today.'

'But you have brought this upon yourself.'

Now he was weeping, 'Please, please!'

Jaiswal could have sent a sub-inspector to the hospital to determine if he was telling the truth. He could have asked the driver where the wife of his master was. But he did not think the man would have lied knowing he would be caught out.

Jaiswal told him, 'Look, you can help save your wife if you tell me the source of this tincture ginger berry racket – where it is being made, and how it is distributed. Everyone says your elder brother is the kingpin; everyone knows that.'

'Yes, sir, I know that, but I am no longer with him and I am not doing it. If you trust me, I will get you what you want as soon as I learn of it.'

Inspector Gopalakrishnan interrupted and said, 'Sir, you should not let him go.'

Jaiswal responded, 'Even if we leave him, where can he go? We can always catch him tomorrow. If he betrays me, and breaks his promise, he will pay for it.'

Then Jaiswal told the man, 'Okay. I am leaving you. I am taking the risk. Once word spreads that you were caught, brought to my office and I let you go, I will get a very bad name. So don't cross me.'

He told Gopalakrishnan to let him go, and the driver and the bottles of inji as well.

'Aiyyah, ungal utharavu' (Your wish, sir), Gopalakrishnan responded. But he didn't look very pleased.

Now and then, they continued to catch some clandestine consignments, but nothing more. Jaiswal knew the trade was still going on, but was hidden better. One and a half months later, an envelope showed up on his desk.

Inside was a hand-drawn map with a couple of roads

marked and named and an arrow pointed to an area off one of the roads saying 'storage godown for tincture ginger berry'. Jaiswal was shocked. The location was barely one and a half kilometres from the camp office where his residence was, on the outskirts of Tuticorin.

He called Muthuraj, the Special Branch inspector, and they drove slowly around the place marked on the map. A high boundary wall ran around the area. There was a big gate which was locked. He asked Muthuraj if he knew who owned this property but he didn't know. At one place, the wall was a little lower and they could see a building inside. They could see some bullock carts as well. It looked like a farmhouse.

How would they proceed now? It was said that Balamurugan, the kingpin, was close to Rajendran, a state minister. The grapevine also had it that they were working to have the new superintendent transferred from Tuticorin before he could do any more damage. This rumour impelled Jaiswal to move quickly. He called Sangram Jangid, an assistant superintendent, fresh out of the Police Academy in Hyderabad, to his office the next day. Jangid was training under Jaiswal. He also called Sub-Inspector Ponnuswamy, who was known for being incorruptible. Jaiswal assembled a team and told them to prepare for a raid.

After dinner that evening, he showed them the map and told them the godown had to be raided at three in the morning. It was midnight already. Austin was also included in the team. Secrecy had to be maintained and no one was to leave the premises before the raid was conducted.

At six thirty or so the phone rang. It was Austin. He told Jaiswal excitedly, 'Sir, sir, very big catch!'

The farmhouse had turned out to be the bottling plant for the tincture ginger berry. It was an open area with sheds and a single-storeyed building with rooms. The raiding party had found underground fermentation tanks where the crew would add ginger to alcohol and let it ferment for weeks. After that, the alcoholic potion would be bottled and sealed.

They found some labourers working there. They had all been brought from Kerala blindfolded in a bus on contract for three months. None of them could leave the compound, which was about four acres. They met no one from outside. However, they were given sumptuous food, even mutton. In the sheds that were their living quarters, they found video cassette recorders and many pornographic video cassettes. The police found more than one lakh bottles that had been filled and were ready to be distributed. In the sheds, there were rooms after rooms of bottles ready to be filled and mountains of empty bottles heaped here and there.

At the bottling plant they were able to confirm that it was indeed Balamurugan who owned it. The police went straight to his house and raided it as well and arrested Balamurugan, his brother and his son. It was around half past four in the morning.

Balamurugan's son was furious. He began shouting at the inspector of the North Police Station, Gopal, who also had been handpicked for the raid.

'Nanri katta naye!' (You, ungrateful dog!), he shouted at him. 'How much money have I given you? You return the favour like this? Every time you wanted money, you came and took it from my father. And now you do this?'

The inspector could find no reply.

The police took all three to the factory. Jaiswal brushed his teeth and quickly rushed to the bottling plant, wearing whatever clothes he could find in his haste. He found them all standing around dejectedly. Balamurugan looked like he was in his late fifties; he was tall, fair, with neatly combed hair.

When Balamurugan saw the superintendent, he told him, 'I have paid everyone.'

'Did you pay me?' Jaiswal asked. Balamurugan kept quiet. 'Then, let's not talk about these things – who you paid, when you paid and how much you paid.'

Later he learnt that Inspector Gopal had been suspended some years ago. During the suspension, he was eligible for only half the salary. For that entire period, Balamurugan had given Gopal the other half of his salary. If there was a marriage in the house of a constable, a mixie or a grinder would arrive at his doorstep without him having asked for it. He paid policemen without them asking for it. Balamurugan had four or five Ambassador cars that he would provide if requisitioned for a VIP. Their petrol tanks would always be filled to the brim; in the dashboard there would always be an envelope with a thousand rupees kept for emergency purposes.

'I have done wrong, so you can arrest me. You can arrest

my brother. But what wrong did my son do? He is not part of it. He is studying for his chartered accountancy. Please let him go,' he pleaded.

Jaiswal looked at Austin who said, 'No, sir. His son is the biggest scoundrel. The way he is abusing Inspector Gopal! We should not tolerate it.'

Jaiswal responded, 'His father is admitting it; the brother is admitting it. He is just a boy. If his father is doing something wrong, how is it his fault? He is not involved. I am requesting you to leave the boy out of it.'

'No, sir,' Austin said. 'Don't get carried away, sir. You always get carried away like this.'

'He is just a boy. I am requesting you. Kindly leave the boy out of it and let him go.'

'I am not for it, sir,' said Austin.

'Okay Austin,' Jaiswal said almost jocularly. 'It is a humble request from me. Tomorrow when you come to me with a request, I can also say no to that, can't I?'

'If you put it like that, sir, it is worse than an order.'

'Please don't put the name of the boy in the charge sheet. And ask him to go away from here.'

Afterwards, the rest were handcuffed and marched all the way to the police station. It must have been nine in the morning.

Photographs were being taken, as were samples for the forensic lab. Jaiswal went and washed up, ate breakfast, and went to the police station afterwards. The press was called in, given photographs and briefed.

It was Jaiswal's second briefing. The first time had been after Dharmarajar's killing. He was in the police station, fielding calls that came in as the news of the raid fanned out. As he was about to leave, a constable came in and whispered in his ear, 'Aiyyah, don't trust anyone. This is too big a man. Once you leave the police station, they can open the lockup and ask him to go.'

Jaiswal ordered the number of guards in the police station to be doubled and ordered two locks to be put in the lockup and gave a key each to Austin and Ponnuswamy. He told them that they were to personally see to it that Balamurugan and his brother remained in the lockup. If they wanted to use the toilet, Jaiswal ordered, they could use the iron bucket inside the cell.

The next day, they had to be produced in the court. By evening, the lawyers had started approaching Jaiswal. He told them to go to the police station. Austin said Balamurugan would surely get bail from the court. In the evening, Jaiswal went to the magistrate's house to request him to remand Balamurugan for fifteen days.

The magistrate said, 'Please don't bring him to the court. It will be very difficult to deny him bail there. All his lawyers will be there. Bring him quietly to my house citing some security reason early in the morning before I go to the court. If you produce him in my house, I will remand him.'

Jaiswal entrusted the DSP with this task.

Next day he searched all the newspapers for news about the raid. Strangely, there was nothing in any of the papers, not a word, except in *Makkal Kural*, a newspaper which had leanings towards the AIADMK. The case went on for years afterwards.

But three months later, Balamurugan came to the camp office. Jaiswal asked him to sit. Balamurugan said he had wanted to stop the business for a long time, but it had become difficult to do so. It suited the politicians and the executives of the politicians, and there was money in it. He thanked Jaiswal for letting his son go. He then took out an invitation card and stood up and handed it over. It was an invitation to the wedding of his son a couple of months later. He wanted Jaiswal to attend.

Jaiswal said he couldn't.

'We are in different social circles and I cannot afford to be seen in your company,' Jaiswal told Balamurugan, who remained standing though he had been asked to sit.

He placed his right hand over his heart and said, 'I give you my word that I will not go back to the inji business. Naan sathiyam panarein. (I solemnly swear.) I will not go back to it.'

Something in the way he said that convinced Jaiswal that he meant it. He responded that since Balamurugan had sworn off the business, he would definitely be there for the wedding. He kept the invitation in the desk drawer. Later, he told his officers of the promise. Many of them laughed when they heard it. 'Nai valai nimutha mudiyathu, saar' (A dog's tail could not be straightened, sir), they pointed out.

'Sir, how can you go to the wedding?' Austin almost shouted. 'You will become an object of ridicule.'

As the date of the wedding approached, it didn't come to Jaiswal's notice that the inji was back in circulation. There was a merchant navy officer, Captain Lal, who had been posted at Tuticorin port. Many times, he came to the superintendent's house for tea or dinner and the Jaiswals had visited Captain Lal at his house as well.

Lal lived in a rented house in the town and he had two children who were the same age as Jaiswal's children. One time Jaiswal rang him up and asked him if he could borrow his vehicle the next day for a few hours. Lal had a Maruti van.

The following morning, Jaiswal drove the van to the kalyana mandapam (wedding hall), wearing a kurta pyjama, just in time for the muhurtham. As he walked into the marriage hall, people were sitting in chairs on both sides, and the rituals were going on. Balamurugan was on the stage with his son and the bride. He spotted the superintendent and without taking the steps that led down from the stage, holding the corner of his veshti (dhoti), he leapt off the stage to come running to greet the guest. He took Jaiswal to the stage to bless the couple by showering them with turmeric-coloured rice and flowers. His son and the bride touched his feet. As he turned around to leave, Balamurugan said, 'Wait a minute,' and went running somewhere and came back with a packet which he thrust into Jaiswal's hand. Jaiswal said he could not accept it. Balamurugan tore the packet to show that it was a veshti with a golden zari border.

'Ulley onnum illaiye?' (Nothing is inside?) Jaiswal asked.

'Ulley onnum illai' (Nothing is inside), he replied. Jaiswal took it and went back to the van to drive back. The man who had been behind the tincture ginger berry racket accompanied him all the way to the van.

It was around this time that the executive director (ED) of SPIC sought an appointment through the public relations officer (PRO) to meet the superintendent. Jaiswal was happy to meet him because senior police officials often used the SPIC guest house.

The PRO said that SPIC Chairman M.A. Chidambaram was coming to Tuticorin and that he would like to pay him a visit.

'Anything official?' Jaiswal enquired.

The ED said that no, that was not the case.

Jaiswal responded that if it wasn't official, he would come and meet him when the chairman came, out of consideration for his age, if nothing else. M.A. Chidambaram was about eighty years old, then. After two days, Jaiswal got a call from him saying that the SPIC chairman was inviting him, his wife and their two children for dinner at the SPIC guest house. Jaiswal was given a date and a time as well.

M.A. Chidambaram was an elderly gentleman. He was there with his wife, who made Jaiswal's daughter sit on her lap and talked to her. Jaiswal asked if there was anything he could do for him.

'No, young man. I wanted to congratulate you. In Madras, there were certain people who were moving around with wads and wads of rupees to get you transferred from here.'

This information coming from the chairman of SPIC stunned Jaiswal. Chidambaram continued, 'I was told that they were ready to pay twenty lakh rupees to have you transferred. MGR had almost said yes. They told the chief minister, "Antha aalluku Tamil theriyathu. Seriya police valai panna mattaar. Makkal kashta padaranga." (That man, the SP, doesn't know Tamil. He doesn't know police works. People are suffering.) "You should post some Tamil-speaking officer to Tuticorin," they had requested.

'It was your DGP, Mr Ravindran, who intervened and told MGR that Anoop Jaiswal was doing very well. But because he is tough, they want him out of there. MGR agreed to let you continue.'

Jaiswal told Chidambaram that if he had been offered half of that amount, he would have gladly left the district and run away himself. (Twenty lakhs in those days would probably be equal to twenty crores now.)

Chidambaram laughed heartily and said, 'Seriya sonnai, seriya sonnai!' (Rightly said, rightly said!)

Shortly afterwards, the secret fund for the Tuticorin police department was raised from one lakh rupees a year to two lakh rupees. When Jaiswal thanked the DGP for his generous donations to the district funds, he said, 'Look at it this way – you brought back the name of Thoothukudi from Injikudi.'

5

Post paid

It was sometime in August or September 1988. Three young men helped an old woman into Superintendent of Police Anoop Jaiswal's room in his camp office. They eased her into a chair and stood behind her. Jaiswal asked what he could do for her. They said that the paati (old woman) was from the village of Pappankulam in Nanganeri taluk. It was a hundred kilometres southwest of Tuticorin, a tough journey for an old woman. She was bent, frail and must have been in her late eighties. Her head was trembling continuously, and when she spoke her voice came out in hesitant quavers and half whispers. She wasn't able to speak coherently and most of the talking was done by one of the three men who accompanied her. They lived in her neighbourhood; they knew the paati.

Jaiswal understood, from what the old lady and the youth said, that about thirty years ago she had leased her one acre of land to her relatives on the promise that they would look after her. Now, she lived in a small hut, which was in urgent need of repairs. When it rained, water leaked into the hut incessantly through the broken roof. Nobody had the time or the inclination to fix the various parts of the hut that had steadily given way. The whole dwelling was in the process of crumbling into the soil it had risen from.

The old woman lived alone, and the previous week she had had a fever but no one brought her medicines. She was left to fend for herself. The relatives, who lived nearby, were supposed to leave food for her every day, but sometimes they forgot. Then she would shuffle, bent over, to their house and beg for food.

From what Jaiswal could make out, it seemed that she had lived far longer than the relatives had expected her to. Now she wanted to get the land back from her relatives. She wanted to then give it to the men who had accompanied her to that station. These people, she said, were sure to look after her, at least better than her own relatives.

There seemed no clear way to proceed in the matter. Jaiswal could call the other party, reprimand them and warn them that if anything happened to the old lady they would be in trouble. He could try and make them see the other point of view. Usually, the intention of the other party was not to be on the wrong side of the law, and mostly they were not criminals either.

Jaiswal asked her if she had any children or other relatives.

'Illai, aiyyah' ('No, sir'), she said. Her voice was hardly louder than a whisper as she struggled to speak.

What about her husband, asked Jaiswal.

'Illai, aiyyah.'

Then, almost accidentally, she said that her husband had been a policeman.

'Policeman? Where?'

She did not know.

'When did he retire?'

'Illai, aiyyah. Poitarru.' (No, sir. He died.)

Jaiswal asked her when he had died.

She looked confused. She talked with the young men, who said that it had happened long before they were born. The oldest of the men looked to be in his mid-thirties. The old woman's husband died when she had been a young woman, over fifty years ago, perhaps. From what Jaiswal could make out, he had died before Independence, before August 1947, over forty years ago. She had given her land to her relatives thirty years ago. That must have been in the late fifties. She didn't have any clear idea of the passing years.

Jaiswal asked her what the name of her husband was. She wasn't able to name him.

'Have you forgotten his name?' Jaiswal asked.

'I haven't forgotten, aiyyah. I have never called my husband by his name,' she replied.

The married women of her generation and social circle were not permitted to utter the name of their spouse.

'How can I help you if you can't tell me his name?' he asked.

'He had the name of Lord Rama's younger brother,' she replied.

'Bharat?'

'No, the other one.'

'Lakshman?'

She nodded.

While this interaction was going on, one of the sub-inspectors, Muthuraj, a bright young man, was also present in the room. He was usually present during such interactions to help in translating because Jaiswal's Tamil was shaky at the time.

'Sir, we can enquire at the village and maybe we can get more details,' Muthuraj said.

Jaiswal was aware that the government had worked out some scheme in the fifties whereby pension was given to people who had worked in the police or government and had to leave for various reasons. He asked Muthuraj how making enquiries at the village would help.

'Sir, based on oral evidence, if we are able to get a death sentence in a murder case, can't we think of some evidence from the village to work out a plan and get pension for her?'

That made sense. He directed that an enquiry be made in her village. He also told Muthuraj to tell the relatives of Ammathai Ammal, for that was her name, in no uncertain terms, that the SP would be very unhappy if something untoward were to happen to the old woman. He sent her away, telling her that he would look into her matter.

The sub-inspector went to her village and made extensive enquiries; some villagers recalled their grandparents telling them that Ammathai's husband had been a policeman, but nothing concrete came out of it. Before filing the report, the sub-inspector went to Ammathai's house and asked her if there was anything she remembered from the time her husband had been alive, anything at all. She could not recall much but she led him into her hut, and by the sunlight that glimmered through the broken tiles and gaps left by the ones that had gone missing through the years, she rummaged slowly through an old aluminium box that had long lost its lustre and finally brought out a cloth bag. It was tied with a thread.

She opened the bag in front of the sub-inspector, fumbling as she did it. Something metallic fell out of it and clattered on the floor. Muthuraj bent and picked it up . It looked like a brass buckle, the kind you find in belts that police personnel wore. How it came to be there, she could not remember. Inside the cloth bag there was also a postcard. It had been folded. She gave it to Muthuraj who opened it. It was a penny postcard. She didn't know what it was. The writing was in Tamil and had faded, because droplets had smudged, but the signature was clear. It was signed in the end by 'Lakshmanan Naidu'.

Then Muthuraj read it out. 'You know I have been working in the police for seven years and how regretful I feel for not being able to have you stay with me. I had not been allotted a house till now. Now, I am posted in Siruvaikundam Police Station. The aivalar sir (sub-inspector) has promised me that a line hut would be falling vacant within three months. So don't worry. Once it is allotted, I will come and get you. Then together we shall live, like the husband and wife we are. We will finally be able to have a family. I pray that happens soon.'

The postmark was smudged. It was a quarter-anna postcard. The year appeared to be 1923.

Muthuraj asked the old woman if the husband had come later to take her to Siruvaikundam.

She said, 'No, he died before he could take me there.'

'How did he die?'

She had no recollection of that. She said there had been news that her husband had died and later his body had been brought to the village for the last rites. Beyond that, she did not remember anything.

The sub-inspector brought the postcard and the buckle to the camp office and Jaiswal took it to the district police office. He called his personal assistant (PA) and asked him if the objects could be the basis for working out a pension. Lakshmanan had, after all, worked for seven years in the force and the letter indicated he had died while still in service.

The PA said, 'Sir, but this is no proof, a postcard like this. To get money from the pension office, more stringent proof will be needed.'

Jaiswal had the archives of the Siruvaikundam police station records searched. There was nothing to show that Lakshmanan had been there; there existed no record of the allotment of the line hut to him either. They could find no corroboration. In the end Jaiswal sent the letter and the buckle through a special messenger to the forensic laboratory in Madras.

Ten days later, the forensic experts were able to determine that the postcard was genuine. If the postcard was genuine, Jaiswal thought, the contents were bound to be genuine as well. He consulted his line head, the DIG in Tirunelveli. The DIG brushed him aside, remarking, 'Jaiswal, don't you have any better work to do than chase ghosts of people who are long dead?'

Jaiswal's PA remained sceptical. He was a gazetted officer and the administrative head of the office. He knew all the rules and regulations and he repeated, 'Sir, this is not going to work.'

'Look, we can try,' Jaiswal proposed. 'Whatever objections you have against my proposal you write it in blue ink. If I overrule it as head of this office in green ink, then it is my responsibility. So, I take that responsibility. You write your objections, and I will overrule it. That way you will not be pulled up for lack of application of mind or for wrongful work.'

Jaiswal sent the letter on to the government, with the objections and his having overruled them, recommending due family pension for Ammathai Ammal. Prompt came the response from the government with the question: 'How can the superintendent of police recommend family pension on such flimsy evidence?' Jaiswal's office was awash with titters and talk about how the SP got carried away too easily.

Jaiswal found it difficult to digest the situation. He was troubled. His ego was hurting, certainly. He was thinking about it when he finally fell asleep. He must have woken up at six in the morning or so and felt surprisingly fresh. Even before taking his first cup of tea, he went straight to his desk at the camp office and started composing a letter.

> Dear Sir,
> In a letter you have termed the evidence flimsy. I am of the opinion that it is the strength of the evidence that is important and not the source of it. And I reiterate and it follows that no crook could have forged such a document in 1923 to cheat the government in 1988.
>
> Second, the letter in question, viz., the penny postcard, was never produced before me by that old hapless lady. It was accidentally discovered by my inspector in the course of the enquiry. Hence, I cannot think of any mala fide intention behind the production of that letter.
>
> Third, as far as I understand, service records are supposed to be permanent records. Failure on the part of the district administration to maintain the records should not be a cause of penalty to a hapless old woman eighty-seven years of age.
>
> Last but not the least, any delay in this matter is likely to cause irreparable damage because at the age of eighty-seven, Ammathai Ammal is living with one foot in the grave.

Jaiswal then went to the district office and asked his PA to prepare his reply on his official letterhead along these lines, giving the reference of the government. He signed the letter and sent it.

A fortnight later, Jaiswal fielded a call from the DGP, Mr Ravindran. 'Congratulations Jaiswal!' were the first words he heard.

'What for, sir? What has happened?'

'Oh, but you are a star!'

'In what way, sir? Surely you are pulling my leg about something!'

'No, Anoop, today the legislators of the Tamil Nadu assembly thumped the desk in your name. It appears that the government has sanctioned the pension for a woman sixty-five years after the death of her husband, and the government took credit for being a very responsive government. Anoop, even the people in the Opposition pointed out that it is because of the efforts of the superintendent of police that this had happened. The entire assembly thumped the desk in appreciation for your work. Apparently, it is a record for this country, perhaps the entire world, even. So, congratulations!'

The very next day Jaiswal received a letter from the government through a special messenger. He was pleasantly surprised. Twenty-two thousand rupees had been sanctioned as arrears for Ammathai Ammal, and there was a cheque for that amount. A family pension of two hundred and ninety-six rupees per month had also been sanctioned.

Jaiswal called Muthuraj, gave him the cheque and the order, and said, 'Please go and get an account opened in her name in a bank. Tell her she will get a pension.'

After Muthuraj had gone away, later that evening, the DIG from Tirunelveli called and congratulated him and made this suggestion: 'Why don't you arrange a function where we call this lady and hand over the cheque?'

'Sir, I have made a mistake again.'

'What have you done now?'

'Sir, I have already sent the order to her and it has been deposited in the bank in her name.'

'Oh, Jaiswal. What have you done? How can you be so thoughtless? This was such a good opportunity for some good publicity for the police. How typical of you to fail even in this.'

6

Spiral

Valliammal worked as a sweeper in Jaiswal's house in Tuticorin. She would come in through the back door, sweep the house, swab it, clean the bathrooms and then go on her way. Neelam mentioned one day to her husband that Valliammal hadn't been coming for three days and had neglected to forewarn her about it. She had not sent a word about how long she would stay away from work either. Jaiswal told her he would see if other arrangements could be made for the work to be done.

He didn't have to. Valliammal was back the next day.

When she was asked why she hadn't come for work, she started weeping. Neelam could not follow what Valliammal was saying, for she spoke hysterically and rapidly. Neelam's Tamil was worse than her husband's, which in turn was barely functional. Neelam told Jaiswal that something was wrong.

Jaiswal summoned Valliammal to the camp office at the

front of the house and asked her what the matter was. She was distraught and the superintendent could not quite catch what she was saying either. However, the constable who was present there was able to decipher Valliammal's words and translated them for Jaiswal. Valliammal's cousin, not a first cousin, but close enough for a relative to be called a cousin, had committed suicide. He had been under pressure to repay a loan to a moneylender.

Jaiswal asked if somebody had beaten him up or forced him to take his own life. Valliammal didn't know the details, but she said her uncle's wife, her chiththi, would know. Jaiswal summoned the Special Branch inspector and told him to talk to the chiththi and find out what had happened.

In the evening, they brought the chiththi to Jaiswal. What she had to say shocked him.

Seven or eight years ago, Valliammal's cousin had taken a loan from a moneylender to meet the expenses for a family function. The amount had been two thousand rupees. He and his wife both were sweepers, and they were paying two hundred rupees as interest per month for those eight years. Whenever they couldn't make the monthly payment for some reason, the interest was added to the principal. The principal was about four thousand rupees, for which they were paying four hundred rupees interest per month. It was a big amount as both their wages together wouldn't have been more than two thousand rupees.

Just a few days before he committed suicide, Valliammal's cousin received news from his brothers living near Maniachi that their father had died. He had left behind a small house to be divided among the three brothers. They had made an evaluation of the house and his share came to forty-three hundred rupees. His two brothers made the proposal that they would together pay Valliammal's cousin that amount, and after that he would have no claim to his share of the house any more. He agreed, and they gave him the money, which he brought home. His wife told him it was a lot of money. More money than they ever got to see at one time. Moreover, it was the amount that they owed the moneylender. She asked her husband to go to the moneylender so that they could have the loan cancelled. It would certainly ease their finances.

Valliammal's cousin went to the moneylender's agent and told him he had four thousand rupees, and he wanted to have the loan cancelled. It was somewhere in the middle of the month, so an interest of two hundred rupees would be there. He told the agent that he would pay forty-two hundred rupees and the loan could be closed.

The moneylender responded, 'Look, this is the month of May and they don't take the principal back in the middle of the year. You can only have that done in December or January to have your loan closed.'

This response stumped Valliammal's cousin and he told the agent, 'If you don't take this money now, it will get spent here and there, and nothing will be left. Ellam selavu ayirum. (Everything will get spent.) And I won't be able to repay.'

The agent then told him that if he feared that it would get

spent, he could leave the money, the four thousand rupees, behind and it would be adjusted against future interest for ten months. In other words, he needn't pay the interest for ten months. From the eleventh month he could resume paying his interest. Valliammal's cousin thought that at least now there would be a respite for eleven months. So, he left the money with the agent and went back to tell his wife the good news.

His wife viewed the development with suspicion. She said, 'No, no, no. We will give him four hundred rupees per month. Get the money back. With four thousand, we can do something ourselves, maybe even lend it out.'

And so Valliammal's cousin ran back to the agent and asked him to return the money. The agent told him that it would not be possible since the amount had already been entered in the books and sent him away saying that he could come back after ten months. There was no arguing with the man.

When he apprised his wife of this development, she chided him and harangued him over his foolishness. Valliammal's cousin went a couple of times more to the moneylender's agent, who then turned belligerent. He couldn't see a way out of the situation. Out of frustration, using his wife's saree, he had hanged himself from a bar in the house.

Jaiswal felt numb hearing the story. His department colleagues, who were also listening, didn't feel anything was out of place. They said many of these people, often drinking their meagre earnings away, borrowed money from such ruthless moneylenders. They had to know what they were getting into. Who in their proper mind would even give them a loan otherwise? Valliammal's cousin had taken a loan knowing the ramifications, and he had known what he was letting himself into.

'No, this is abetment to suicide,' Jaiswal interjected. 'The moneylender, through this agent, has wrongly harassed him and because of his harassment, which became unbearable, the man committed suicide.'

It was with reluctance that the policemen agreed to register a case. Then Jaiswal wanted to know how many people were caught in this situation. In Tuticorin, there were two harbours, and a large number of manual labourers and workers, both men and women, were employed for various tasks such as sweeping, cleaning, lifting loads, etc. They often found themselves out of cash.

If they took a loan of a hundred rupees, they would have to pay an interest of ten rupees every month. Any month when there was failure to pay the ten rupees, it would be added to the principal. For four months, if ten rupees is paid, and in the fifth month there is failure to pay, the moneylender will not even insist, he will say, Never mind, it is all right. Don't worry. From the next month, pay eleven rupees per month. Just one rupee more.

The principal amount, then, would become hundred and ten and ten per cent of hundred and ten is eleven, and so the interest became eleven rupees. Paththu vatti. (Ten per cent.) That was why the system was widely known because it was also widely practised. No one thought it was wrong or even odd. It was a way of life.

In the harbour, Jaiswal learnt that right at the counter, where the monthly or weekly payments were made to the labourers, the moneylenders and their collection agents would be standing with a list. And the man who was paying the labourer's wages would himself deduct the interest and pay the wages minus the interest to the labourer, and the interest would go to the collection agent. In the end, the accountant would get a small commission for his efforts. Everyone got their share. This was the accepted norm. This was the story all over the district. It was extortion, in plain sight, yet no one saw it that way.

There was an act on moneylending that prohibited charging interest more than two per cent per month. Its cognizance was under the Revenue Department and not with the police. When you join the police force as an ASP, the focus is on traditional crime, which authorities or seniors review – crimes such as murder, murder for gain, dacoity, theft and the like.

Jaiswal found it incongruous that if there was a theft of fifty thousand rupees in a house, the police would move fast, but if a person was cheated of five lakh rupees it would be taken up much less enthusiastically because crimes like cheating did not get reviewed by seniors. It was not something that was reflected in performance statistics.

Here the man had committed suicide even though he had the wherewithal to close the loan, and he was unscrupulously not allowed to do so because of his and his wife's ignorance, which had been exploited. Undoubtedly, there had to be many others like him.

Information started pouring in. Jaiswal started chasing the moneylender's agents, who also acted as bouncers. Most of them were well built, hefty and went around riding 350cc red Royal Enfield Bullets. They would park the Bullet by the counter where the wages would be distributed. On payment day, Jaiswal posted police at these spots with the order that no agents of moneylenders or bouncers should be allowed in the vicinity when the wages were being distributed.

So ignorant were the people that they did not even know how to calculate interest and figure out how much they owed. It was the word of the moneylender that was final. Sweepers and labourers maintained no books or calculations in their houses. There was no supervision over what the moneylenders were doing.

When the figures were collated, sheet after sheet, with the initial loan and where the amount stood now, the documents made for a chilling read. In one instance, a person had been paying interest not for one or two years, or even seven or eight years, but sixteen years. He was still paying. He would continue to pay till he died. The initial loan had been of a thousand rupees. The interest paid so far was sixty-four thousand rupees. People were paying endlessly. Many who couldn't pay any more left the town and disappeared.

There were two moneylenders who caught Jaiswal's

attention. One was Christopher. He owned a shipping agency. The other one was Lakshmanan, the brother-in-law of the municipal councillor. Lakshmanan worked in the municipal areas, and Christopher, in the areas around the harbour. Jaiswal had extortion cases registered in the Tuticorin North and South Police Stations against them.

When he brought the issue to the collector's notice, he was told that there were very few moneylenders who were registered. Most of this business was conducted unregistered. Over four months, Jaiswal was able to gather the records of about sixteen hundred people who found themselves in that helpless spiral of the increasing principal.

There was a chief minister's conference of collectors and SPs where Jaiswal made a presentation detailing the menace of moneylending. He made the suggestion that if the Money Lending Act was made more cognizable, it would allow for ruthless eradication of the practice. Someone asked, 'Where will these poor souls go for money then? Who would stand surety for the collateral?'

Jaiswal met the income tax commissioner in Madras, who directed him to Mr Selvaraj, the deputy commissioner of income tax, based in Madurai.

Jaiswal went and met Mr Selvaraj. He was young and enthusiastic but pointed out that Christopher was a big troublemaker as well. As far as rowdyism went, Jaiswal told Mr Selvaraj, he could take care of it because there was no rowdy bigger than himself, for the simple reason that as an SP, he had more men and arms at his command than any lout could possibly have. Jaiswal told him he could handle that part. But he was helpless at the financial part. The SP had no powers there. That is where he wanted the help of the Income Tax Department.

Jaiswal's intelligence wing had built a dossier on both Christopher and Lakshmanan – their activities, details of their properties and their benamis. He asked Mr Selvaraj whether a raid could be conducted on those two people, to unearth any ledger that showed the number of people who were struggling in their clutches. Mr Selvaraj said, 'Please, keep it a secret, but I will be happy to help. I will inform you.'

A fortnight later, Jaiswal received a call from Mr Selvaraj. It was a Friday. Mr Selvaraj asked, 'Can we organize a raid on Monday? I am sending about forty people from the Income Tax Department, but I need police support.'

'How many men?' Jaiswal asked.

Mr Selvaraj said at every place he was going to raid, he needed two or three policemen, and in the houses of Christopher and Lakshmanan, senior officers were required to be present. Jaiswal agreed and mobilized his armed reserve constabulary.

Mr Selvaraj came on Sunday and stationed himself at the SPIC guest house. Jaiswal went there to finalize the details. He formed eighteen police parties to go with the income tax raid party.

The raids started simultaneously in eighteen locations before the sun could even come up on Monday. All of Monday, the raids continued. Sometime on Tuesday, Jaiswal learnt that the income tax officials had seized, among other things, from Christopher's premises, eleven hundred blank stamp papers which either had the signature or thumb impressions and the names of people who had been lent money. It left Christopher the leeway to fill the stamp papers any way he wanted. These blank stamp papers gave him the power he wielded over the people he had lent money to and whom he exploited.

'What should I do with them?' Mr Selvaraj asked.

'Burn them all, Mr Selvaraj. Burn them all,' Jaiswal told him.

Jaiswal, incidentally, remembered that any confession made to a police officer was inadmissible in court. But any admission made to an income tax official by any assessor could be recorded and used as a confession.

He requested Mr Selvaraj to, in the course of his interactions with Christopher and Lakshmanan, get statements from both of them, regarding the number of people who owed them money as loans. Later, Mr Selvaraj told Jaiswal that both of them had said that nobody owed them any money. Not one person owed them money as loans. They were made to furnish statements to that effect as well. Jaiswal requested Mr Selvaraj for copies of this statement duly authenticated. He had those statements distributed in the harbour areas and in the municipal areas, all over, and asked the sweepers and the labourers to keep the copy safely. It was proof that they owed no one any money any longer.

It was on an early morning some three months later when some fifteen or twenty people came to the camp office and began making a small ruckus. Hearing their shouts, Jaiswal asked what it was all about.

They were all sweepers and labourers from the harbour area. They said that in the early hours, three or four people rode in on red Bullet motorcycles and called the people out of their houses to ask, 'Yethannai naal than intha SP inga iruppan? (How many days do you think this SP will remain here?) He will get transferred. We will get him transferred. We will burn down your homes after he is gone. You think the police will help you then? If you don't pay the money that you owe us, you will all be finished. We will somehow get the money back. With interest.'

Somehow, it was portrayed as if the raids and what had followed had happened due to the act of one individual and that it was an aberration. The crowd assumed that once the individual was out of the scene, there would be nobody to protect them. It didn't occur to them that the police department, as one unit, was helping them. Jaiswal could see that among those who had come to him, there were several well-built people as well.

He turned around and shouted to the guard, 'Put your rifle aside and get me a big lathi – the biggest you can find, the strongest you can find.'

The guard went inside the guardhouse and came out with five or six lathis, which he held out to Jaiswal, asking him, 'Aiyyah, yethu venam?' (Sir, which one?). Jaiswal carefully examined the lathis and chose two. Then he instructed the guard to separate the women from the men and bring the men over to him.

The guard told the women to stand back and asked the men to come forward and stand in a group. There were fifteen or so men. There was some consternation as to what was going to happen.

'I want you to beat these rascals with the lathis,' Jaiswal instructed the guard. 'Beat them till the first lathi breaks, and then use the other to beat them until the other lathi also breaks. Thrash these fellows!'

The guard was shocked. 'Aiyyah, what if they are hurt badly?'

'I want them to get a thrashing they will not forget. They should have marks to show their grandchildren, so don't go easy on the beating. And one more thing, don't ever allow these worthless rascals to come anywhere near here again.'

'Why are you having us beaten, sir? What have we done?' one of the visitors asked.

'I am having you beaten because you deserve it,' Jaiswal responded. 'Yerumai madu mathiri thala kizhe vechutu, yen kitta odi vaaringa? Ungalay ellam Kadavul kooda kaapatha mudiyathu. (Two or three people come to your locality, threaten hundreds of you staying there, and you, like dumb buffaloes, come running to me with your heads down.Even God cannot save you.) I am not saying kill those agents of the moneylenders. But I expected after what had happened that you would at least catch them, give them a beating, bind them and bring them here. But no, you are worse than buffaloes.'

'Aiyyah namba ippadi panna namba mela case varum?' (But sir, if we do that, won't there be cases against us?)

'There will be no cases against you, if that happens. You have my word. But you also have my word that the next time you come like this, like buffaloes, or dogs with your tails between your legs, I myself will beat you.'

Four days later the SP was again drawn by a commotion outside. There stood a line of rickshaws outside the camp office compound. They were filled with labourers and sweepers. All of them looked jubilant. In one of the rickshaws, two persons were sitting, bound in ropes and bleeding from the beating they had received. They looked confused, as though they couldn't fathom what had hit them.

7

The Thief of Nazareth

In the Siruvaikundam subdivision of Tuticorin, there was a police station in Nazareth. In the late eighties, it was a quiet part of the district with a population of not more than four thousand people. Nothing of consequence ever happened there that brought the Nazareth police station to the attention of the superintendent of police.

Then, suddenly, Nazareth started to often feature in the crime meetings that were held every month. This happened after the Tamil Nadu government began providing free meals to children attending schools, to make it an incentive for them to come to school, as well as to ensure that there was uniformity in nutrition.

The scheme later went on to cover elderly people and lactating mothers. Noon meal centres were opened all across the state, and lakhs of children ate their lunch at school, especially those from the poorer strata of society whose parents were too poor to provide three meals a day regularly.

There was a special direction to the district officers, the district collectors and district superintendents of police to ensure that these centres functioned properly and effectively, by providing good meals to the beneficiaries and that there was no pilferage there.

Nazareth came to the notice of Jaiswal after a series of thefts at the noon meal centres and ration shops within the station limits and in the neighbouring areas. To prepare food in the schools for the noon meal, rice, lentils, Bengal gram, green gram, palmolein oil and salt, and later on as they were added to the menu, boiled eggs and vegetable were stored. These thefts of oil, grains and rice were reviewed in the crime meetings and the deputy superintendent of police and the inspector of the area were asked to ensure that these crimes were immediately checked. Yet, they continued, without any signs of letting up.

Forensic experts who were sent to the scenes of the crimes discovered that in many of the thefts, the fingerprints that they lifted from the locks and doors happened to be the same. In the police database, they matched a KD, a Known Delinquent or Known Desperado, called Swathantra Balan.

A team was formed within the station limit to nab him. Not much was known about him, except that he was in his late twenties, and that he had been involved in petty crimes and thefts, not violent felonies. He had been convicted and let off on parole for juvenile crimes. In the subsequent crime meeting, Jaiswal made the point that it was strange that a known criminal was at large stealing with impunity and abandon, while the police stood by and watched helplessly.

A few days later he heard a story about Balan.

One day, three constables had been on night patrol on the streets of Nazareth, and on the verandah of a small shopping complex, they found a person sleeping on the footpath, covered with a sheet. As a routine to ascertain the identity of such people, one of the constables tapped his lathi on the ground near the face of the sleeping person. The person continued to sleep. The constable then prodded the sleeping form. By now the three policemen had crowded around the sleeping form. When the prodding continued more vigorously, the sleeping person sat up and found himself surrounded by policemen. He was surprised, and so were the police.

The policemen were immediately able to recognize him as Swathantra Balan. But before the policemen could grab him, he had thrown his sheet over them, pushed them aside, slipped past them and had disappeared into the darkness.

The pressure on the Nazareth police station continued.

They now knew that Balan was prowling in the area. Then, one day there was a message that he had been arrested. After the way the KD had been able to give three constables the slip, Jaiswal was surprised that Balan had even been arrested.

He told the DSP, Pratap Singh, that the constable who arrested him should be rewarded. Pratap Singh told him it was not a constable who had made the arrest, but the station sub-inspector, Manivannan, who had single-handedly arrested the KD.

'Really? Manivannan? He directly, personally and single-handedly arrested the KD, this Swathantra Balan?'

Pratap Singh laughed, and said, 'Yes, sir. Our Manivannan!'

Manivannan, Jaiswal recalled, was a nice person but very slow when it came to physical activity. He was the kind of person who, slowly and with difficulty, followed his paunch around. When he attempted to get up from his chair, it was like watching a slow-motion clip. He was much faster in writing records and investigation diaries or attending courts. But physical activity wasn't his thing.

No, it must have been some other constable who had done it, and Manivannan was just taking the credit, Jaiswal thought. Just find out who arrested Balan, he ordered. It can't be Manivannan.

The DSP made his enquiries and came back, saying, 'No, sir. It was Manivannan who arrested Balan. Personally. No one else.'

Jaiswal said, 'Okay. That is very interesting. We have heard so much about this KD of Nazareth. Why don't we call him in here. I would like to talk to him before we send him on remand.'

Three hours later, Balan was in Jaiswal's office. The DSP was present there too. Jaiswal offered Balan a chair, and he sat down with some hesitation. He appeared very agile, slim and toughly built. There was so much innocence in his face that Jaiswal could not believe that this was the infamous KD who had eluded the police for months.

'How did you get arrested?'

'I will not be beaten?' Balan asked first.

'Why should anyone beat you?'

'Please assure me that I will not be beaten.'

'No one is going to beat you,' Jaiswal assured him and ordered that tea be served.

While they waited for the tea to arrive, Balan told Jaiswal about himself. He had lost his parents early in his life. He didn't remember anything about them and had grown up in a village near Nazareth. He had been a ringleader in a small way, stealthily plucking fruit , stealing vegetables or eggs from other people's orchards and pens, with his band of friends. He grew up committing petty crimes, which were often not reported.

Many nights he found shelter in the cathedral, doing odd jobs of sweeping, cleaning and running errands for the priests. Sometimes they fed him, and he began attending church. When he was fourteen, he had been arrested for some crime to which he had confessed and so was let out on parole as he was a juvenile and because of his good behaviour. When he was older, at twenty-one, he was arrested yet again for some other petty offence; he confessed and spent six months in Palayamkottai Jail, not far from Nazareth.

Jaiswal asked him about the noon meal centre thefts.

'Sir, I have not committed all the thefts. Some I did, but most I did not.'

'What do you mean? Your fingerprints are all over the locks.'

'I don't deny I had a hand in breaking the locks. But in how many of these thefts have you found my fingerprints, other than on the locks, the bolts and the doors? In how many instances were they found inside the rooms?'

'How do you explain this then?' asked Jaiswal.

'Sir, I can get by most times without having to steal. The church has been good to me. God has been kind. Many times, sir, the authorities who run these noon meal places send for me and ask me to break the lock of the storeroom. I do it, sir, whenever they ask me to do it. And they give me some money to break the lock. That's all. I go away with the money they have given me. Nothing else.'

'Why do they want you to break the locks?'

'I am good at breaking locks, sir.'

'Yes, but why break the locks?'

'I don't ask questions, sir. I don't like to get beaten up. But, I will tell you what I have heard, if you don't beat me.'

'What is it?'

'I hear, sir, that the Revenue Department has got a new officer. He is very strict with the provisions and the storage in the noon meal centres. He has made it difficult for the noon meal people to steal the oil or rice or paruppu (lentils), sir. I think I am getting too much credit for the thefts.'

'The ration shop thefts?'

'Not me, sir. I just broke the locks.'

'Then why is your name in the police records so many times?'

'Sir, the police beat me and ask me to confess to crimes I have not committed. I confess, sir. I don't want to be beaten up or tortured. I can't bear it. I confess, sir, when I am asked to. It is easier that way. I do not like the beatings.' Balan left the superintendent's room happy that he had not been beaten and even happier that the SP had given him a cup of tea. Strange are the ways of the Lord, he said as he left Jaiswal's office with a smile.

After Balan left, Jaiswal summoned Sub-Inspector Manivannan and chided him for inflating his record. He told him to record the confession of KD Balan without embellishment, so that it could be forwarded to the Revenue Department. They could, then, do an enquiry on how the provisions kept disappearing.

A better picture of how Sub-Inspector Manivannan arrested Balan came to light later when Jaiswal made enquiries.

It had been the Thursday before Easter. Balan had gone to St John's Cathedral for Eucharist Mass, which celebrates the occasion of the Last Supper, where Jesus washed the feet of his disciples to clean them, for he knew one of them was soon going to betray him. In the meal, Jesus offered them his flesh and blood in the form of bread and wine.

Balan was in the cathedral when a police spotter had seen him. The spotter ran to the Nazareth police station to inform the head constable, whom he knew and to whom he regularly gave information. When the spotter reached the station, the head constable was not there. He was preparing to leave the place, when in the doorway the large, corpulent frame of Sub-Inspector Manivannan confronted him and blocked his way.

'Who are you?' Manivannan had asked brusquely. The other thing about Manivannan was that he could never manage to speak softly. He always yelled. He followed up the first question with a second, even louder, one, 'What do you want?' When the spotter failed to answer, fearing the repercussions, Manivannan had thundered, 'Are you dumb? Who do you want to see?'

The spotter mentioned he had come to see the head constable

'Why?' Manivannan relentlessly followed up. Then the spotter blurted to the sub-inspector that Balan was at the St John's Cathedral for the Holy Thursday Mass. Sub-Inspector Manivannan asked the spotter to wait and went into his room to change into his uniform. Manivannan's getting into a police uniform was a laborious, slow and methodical process. The spotter feared that the Mass would be over by the time the sub-inspector emerged dressed formally to make the arrest.

Finally, the sub-inspector came out, adjusted his cap, picked up his revolver and placed it in the holster. With the spotter by his side, he stepped out of the old police station that sat yellowed and low on the side of the Nazareth main road and began his slow, ponderous march to St John's Cathedral, about a kilometre down the same road, where it met Sannidhi Street.

It took a little less than twenty-five minutes for Sub-Inspector Manivannan to lumber into the cathedral, whose spire reached high into the sky, dominating the flatlands that lay all around, broken only by a small body of water in the far distance. By then, Manivannan's uniform had blotches of sweat that had broken out from the exertion of walking the gruelling kilometre.

Through the wide-open doors of the cathedral came the sound of Mass being read. The cathedral was overflowing with people, and they were saying 'Amen!' in one voice when the priest said, 'May the Almighty Lord have mercy on us and forgive us our sins.'

On the table that symbolized the Last Supper, the priest was about to break the holy bread to offer communion, when Manivannan peremptorily beckoned to the spotter, asking him where Balan, was. He began stomping up and down the aisle, which was covered in a red dhurrie all the way to the pulpit. As he peered around trying to locate Balan, the sub-inspector looked like a wild tusker that had suddenly found itself in a crowded street, and when he couldn't locate the offender he called to the spotter who then pointed out Balan from among the kneeling Holy Thursday congregation.

Twice, Sub-Inspector Manivannan caught hold of the wrong man by the collar. Each time a commotion ensued, and the priest studiously ignored the disruption and continued the Mass. The third time the spotter pointed to a kneeling man, Manivannan slowly, carefully, panting a little, manoeuvred himself behind him and managed to catch Balan by his collar.

The KD offered no resistance. He didn't try to run away. All he requested from Sub-Inspector Manivannan was that he be allowed to sit down behind him till the time the Mass was over, following which he would go with Manivannan wherever he wanted him to go. Manivannan would not have any of it. The fact that Balan had given as many as three of his constables the slip weighed heavily on his mind, and he immediately sought the help of three people from the congregation to help him with the arrest, saying, 'This man is a criminal, a thief! Help me arrest him.'

When he shouted the word 'thief' the priest looked towards the commotion and could no longer continue. Sub-Inspector Manivannan led the KD out of the cathedral and took him to the police station. Balan's repeatedly cried out his only request while being taken all the way to the police station – 'Please don't beat me! I am ready to confess to anything you want!'

Jaiswal had asked Balan if he had seen Manivannan coming to catch him. He said yes, he had seen the sub-inspector and had watched him catch two other people before he let them go.

'Why didn't you run away? You are good at that, aren't you? You had ample time and opportunity to run away, right?'

'I wanted to, sir, but I was in the middle of Holy Thursday Mass and I was praying. I wanted to complete my prayer. So, I continued to remain at prayer, leaving my fate to the Almighty Lord.'

To Jaiswal, it seemed Balan's submission to Christ was

complete. He was a true disciple. A criminal? He was not so sure now. Oh yes, that spotter and Balan had been part of the same childhood gang, stealing from orchards and fields when they were children.

That was the connection.

8

The Punnakayal Massacre

Fishermen are a closely knit community.

Superintendent of Police Anoop Jaiswal found this out the hard way, on a road that runs along the coast through Tuticorin district, all the way to Kanyakumari.

Along the road, there were big fishing villages like Periathalai in the Nanganeri subdivision and Punnakayal in Manapad. Most of the fishermen were Christian Nadars, or Christians. Christianity had come to their shores long before the British arrived. Even before you came upon a village, you could spot the church spire. The church played a dominant role in the life of the fishermen.

On Sunday, there was no fishing.

At night, fishermen would set off in their catamarans to lay out nets in the sea. Their fishing depended on boats sailing out into the sea with the land breeze and coming back when the sea breeze blew into the land. They went out in groups. No catamaran was left alone. There would be twenty, thirty or as many as forty catamarans on the water, parallel to each other. There would be six or seven fishermen in each catamaran, laying their nets out in the sea.

It was a task that demanded dexterity and skill. The nets were kept neatly folded, weights on one end and buoys on the other. It would have to be picked up fold-wise, unfurled and laid in the water so it remained suspended for the fish to swim into. If it wasn't laid out properly then the night would be ruined, with just a messy tangle of ropes and wires, and frayed tempers to show for. There would be no fish to sell. It was arduous pulling the net with the fish thrashing alive and folding it afterwards.

The Fisheries Department routinely gave out guidelines on where the boats with outboard motor could fish and where they could not. Nearer to the shore, where the catamarans laid out their nets, was off limits to boats with outboard motors. Off limits too was that part of the sea where the adjacent village fished. Fishing boats with outboard motors had to go further out into the sea to fish. When these boats headed out, on many occasions, the propellers would get entangled in the nets laid out by fisherman in catamarans. Those nets then would have to be cut.

Sometimes motorboats sneaked into catamaran waters chasing large shoals of fish. Sometimes they used the outboard engine to deliberately cut the net to deny the catamaran fishers a bigger catch. This usually happened when the boats fished out of their own turf, in the waters of the adjacent district where their authorities couldn't act on them.

For a fisherman, the fishing net and his catamaran were his most precious possessions, his source of livelihood. If the net was cut, there would be fights and bloodshed. Sometimes when youngsters raced their motorboats for the thrill, the nets would get cut inadvertently. In such cases, catamarans would immediately surround the motorboat. If the fishermen managed to catch the perpetrator, the outboard motor that cut the net would be removed and thrown into the sea. Sometimes, the fishermen held the men on the motor boat as hostages until they received compensation.

Once there was a quarrel between Periathalai village and the adjacent village, which fell in Tirunelveli district, over fishing nets. Some villagers from Periathalai had been held hostage. Jaiswal had sent the deputy superintendent of police, Pratap Singh, to negotiate their release and to ensure that no one came to harm, and no property was destroyed.

Jaiswal had gone to Thiruchendur for a holiday with Neelam and his children. They were staying in the temple guest house. In Thiruchendur, the wireless reception was patchy and so poor that Jaiswal could not contact Pratap.

It was afternoon, around 2 p.m. when Jaiswal told Neelam to wait in the guest house at Thiruchendur and asked the driver to head for Periathalai. It was about twenty-eight kilometres away. Jaiswal initially thought that by then, the matter would have been resolved.

Since he was on a personal holiday, he was not in uniform. As they took the turn off the main road to Periathalai, some forty minutes later, they saw a big crowd of people, mostly women, children and some young men, who were shouting and wailing. Seeing the police car, they converged on it and began throwing sand on the car. The driver had to slow down.

Jaiswal wanted to tell the driver to drive through the crowd and get away from the frenzy. But by then they had surrounded the car. There were too many people and soon the flag was pulled away from the bonnet and the flagstaff deliberately bent. They were thumping on the bonnet, the boot and the door. For a while, Jaiswal couldn't move. He always carried a weapon – at first a 9mm pistol, but it had been too heavy. Now, he carried a much smaller and lighter .38 revolver in a bag. Jaiswal pulled out that bag and held it in his hand. There was only shouting and the sound of sand and pebbles hitting the car and its windshield. Finally, when the car didn't move for a while, the shouting abated.

Jaiswal stepped out of the car and stood clutching his bag with the revolver. The villagers were angry that the hostages hadn't been released yet. Jaiswal said that he had sent a team to secure their release, and that they needed to be patient. He had come there to oversee the situation and make sure that the hostages were set free. But the villagers said that they would hold him hostage until they knew no harm had befallen the prisoners.

'Okay', Jaiswal said. 'I will remain here. I came here only to help you. Now that I am here, at least give me a chair to sit on while we wait.'

A chair was brought and Jaiswal placed it at some distance from the car. When he sat down, they began talking, all at the same time, and he said, 'Why don't you tell me one by one? I am not going anywhere. I can't hear all of you at the same time – please don't shout all at once.'

Jaiswal asked his driver to contact DSP Pratap Singh and find out what was happening. The youngsters in the crowd began to tell him stories of their experiences with the police and other incidents that had no bearing on the situation at hand. At that point, the driver came back and said he was not able to make contact as the wireless reception was very weak. Then Jaiswal told the people they should at least let his car go to a spot where the reception was better so that he could contact the deputed team.

Initially, they were reluctant, but he pointed out that he, as the SP, was there with them as collateral, anyway. In fact there was no better collateral the fisherfolk could hope for in the entire district. The crowd agreed, and the car managed to drive away. It must have been about half past four and the sun had softened. As they waited, the people began to run short of complaints to make; Jaiswal took the opportunity to ask the youngsters how they liked the new outboard engines. He was told that Periathalai had some fibreglass boats as well, fitted with outboard engines. Jaiswal looked out at the sea, calm and endless, and suggested they show him what it felt to ride the waves in a fibreglass boat. He also requested that since he was their guest, if they could get him and the driver, when he came back with news, some dinner. How about some simple meen kolambu (fish gravy), from the hosts? Four young men took Jaiswal to a fibreglass boat that was in the sand beyond the waterline and pushed it into the water. They all got into it, and headed out to sea. He asked how much fuel there was in the boat. They replied that the tank was full.

A hundred yards or so out in the sea, one of the youngsters started abusing the police. Jaiswal guessed the youngster had had a few run-ins with the police and was worked up about it. Now that there was a policeman sitting in the boat, he was venting out his grievances.

'Now that you are in the sea alone with us, we can dump you in the sea. What can you do?'

Jaiswal said with a smile, 'Oh, you are becoming so cheeky! You really want to know?'

Jaiswal pulled out the revolver from the bag and, still smiling, said, 'Look this has five rounds. There are only four of you. I am a good shooter. The four of you will be in the water before me. I will take the motorboat and head straight for Tuticorin.'

Seeing the revolver, the bravado of the young man evaporated. A slightly older, more sensible man said, 'Illai, aiyyah, thappa yeduthukaathinga. Avan chinna payan, kindala pesitaan. Avalavu thaan.' (Don't take it to heart, sir. He is a young boy and was only joking.)

'It's a good thing that I was also joking,' Jaiswal responded, still smiling. He didn't put the revolver back in the bag. Their enthusiasm for the joyride had vanished. At that time, they could see that a crowd had gathered on the beach and they appeared to be gesturing to them to come back. Only as they drew nearer did Jaiswal finally put the revolver away.

He could see his driver in the crowd. Even before he could get off the fibreglass boat, the driver shouted that he had been able to talk to DSP Pratap Singh. The matter had been settled and the hostages were on their way back in a van. Almost at the same moment, two motorcycles arrived, and the same message was given to the villages. And in no time, the people started apologizing and said that they never meant to harm him.

'Then how did my vehicle get damaged?' Jaiswal asked.

The crowd immediately collected some money and gave it to the driver to have the car repaired. They also brought some fish for them. They were now meek and calm. The fisherfolk mirrored the moods of the sea – one moment they were calm and the next, there was no telling what they might do in their fury.

Once, a brother was involved in the kidnapping of his sister's husband. Jaiswal asked him, 'How can you hold your own brother-in-law hostage?'

He simply said that the village was more important to him than his sister. His sister had married out of the village. If someone from their village appeared weeping before the village elders, saying they had been beaten up by men from another fishing village, the people in his village would not hesitate to pick up their weapons. Seldom would a fight within the same village escalate into something serious. The interests of the village always came first.

In another instance, Jaiswal was called to a fishing village where a fisherman, in his anger, had brought down a heavy sickle, wide and curving like the bow of a catamaran, on the shoulder of another fisherman. The blow had been so strong the sickle cut clean through the shoulder blade, scapula, sternum and four of his ribcage bones while coming to rest against the fifth. The victim slumped to the ground, split wide open, his shoulder and left arm cleaved open along with a portion of his chest. One blow was all it took. The sickle must have been sharp and the man who dealt the blow must have had great strength.

It was only through word of mouth that the inspector of Kulashekhara police station got to know of the murder. He took four constables and went to the scene of the crime, a fishing hamlet close to Periathalai, took possession of the body and sent it for post-mortem. A murder case was registered, but no one in the village came forward to say what had happened or who had done it or why the crime had been committed. They claimed that no one had seen anything.

Again, it was through a rumour that the inspector came to know who the attacker was; a team went to arrest the man and take him in for questioning. It was important to recover the murder weapon. The moment he entered the hamlet for this purpose, the inspector faced heavy opposition from the fishermen, more so from the women of the village. They blocked the way, levelling false allegations that the inspector was misbehaving with the women. They wouldn't allow the police to enter the village. The inspector finally withdrew.

The police wanted the accused to surrender. Word

regarding this had been sent through the tehsildar, the Revenue Officer and the Fisheries Department, which usually kept in touch with the villagers because they supplied them with kerosene and helped them in disputes about fishing in other areas.

After a fruitless wait for a couple of days, a peace committee meeting was organized to check the allegations that had been levelled against the inspector. Jaiswal participated in it. At the meeting, a woman was very vocal, explaining vividly how the inspector had tried to tear her blouse and molest her. A very old woman with several of her teeth missing, she tried to demonstrate how the inspector had removed her saree, grabbed her blouse and torn it apart. The allegations made no sense. There, in full daylight, as a crowd looked on, a young inspector, who had gone with a team of five other policemen; how could it be true? What was the motive? What was the purpose? And right in the heart of the village? Why should the inspector go and tear the blouse of a toothless elderly woman? To put pressure on the villagers, their kerosene supply was cut and they found it difficult to run their boats and go out to the sea to fish.

Three days later, a person from the village came carrying an aruval. He had brought along some villagers with him and claimed that he was the accused and that he had come to surrender. Looking at him, DSP Pratap Singh began to laugh.

The person who had come to surrender was a thin old man. Pratap had a stout bamboo placed in front of the old man and asked him to cut it into two with his sickle, telling him, 'If you are able to cut this into two, I will accept that you are the murderer.' The old man stood undecided and looked at the fishermen, who urged him to cut the bamboo pole. The old man feebly went at the pole with his aruval for four or five minutes and still couldn't get the job done.

Then Pratap pulled him aside and asked him, 'Why are you doing this? Somebody has killed someone, but why are you surrendering?'

The old man said, 'I am an old man. You can hang me, it is all right. Already one working man of the village is dead. If we give the name of the person who killed him, you are going to hang him. The village will be short of two able-bodied men. What is the advantage of that? How does our village gain?'

Later, though the accused was arrested, they couldn't recover the weapon. And no one was willing to testify that he had done it. He was remanded for some time, but the case ended with the word Undetected – UN – in the police ledger, which meant that the murderer's identity could not be established.

A few days after the murder, the police learned that the village had held a panchayat where it had been decided that the boat of the assailant was to be handed over to the wife of the victim. There was no greater loss to a fisherman than the loss of his boat. The widow already had her husband's boat. Now, she owned two boats. The assailant was ordered to work for the woman on that boat that was no longer his.

That was the punishment. He worked for three years for her, and then she married him and he became a stepfather to her two sons.

Punnakayal is the largest fishing village on that stretch of the coast, forty-five kilometres from Tuticorin. The Thamarabarani river empties itself into the sea near Punnakayal via a large estuary and is dammed in various places. So, except when the dam water is released in large quantities, the river runs as a thin trickle for the village people to draw water from it, to bathe in it and for the cattle to graze the streamside pastures. Upriver, closer to Tirunelveli, around Ambasamudram and all along the riverbed, green paddy fields stretch as far as the eye can see. The road from Punnakayal to Athoor, the nearest big market, is narrow and runs through Senthamangalam, an Adi Dravidar Harijan village.

There could not have been more than two hundred people living in the village. Senthamangalam and Punnakayal lived in a constant state of tension. Petty quarrels often escalated. In policing terms, there was always a law and order situation in the area.

Jaiswal was aware that a panchayat had been called by the deputy collector, who had wanted the village elders from both settlements to sort out their rivalry in the presence of the tehsildar. The local inspector and the DSP were already there.

This is what had happened. Early in the morning of 23 November 1987, a truck carrying the day's catch from

Punnakayal had been on the road to Athoor where the fish was to be sold. It had hit an Adi Dravidar youth. It was an accident. The youth was injured and the truck was immediately surrounded and blocked by the Adi Dravidars.

Part of that road ran along a bund on the Thamarabarani. It was a pucca road laid years ago and was wide enough to allow traffic only one way. If a vehicle came from the opposite direction, it would have to manoeuvre against the rise of the bund to allow the incoming vehicle to pass. Behind the truck that had been stopped, the other vehicles carrying fish from Punnakayal to the Athoor fish market waited.

The injuries that the youth had suffered when the truck hit him were grave. He was taken to the nearest clinic in a rickshaw. By the time the rickshaw reached the clinic, the youth had died. The infuriated Adi Dravidars attacked the trucks and the vans. The drivers and those fishermen accompanying them fled, leaving their vehicles behind. When word of the standoff reached Punnakayal, the fishermen realized that the day's catch would not make it in time for the auction in Athoor from where the fish was to be sent to other markets.

Rumours spread to the effect that the entire catch had been looted, and the trucks burnt. The fishermen of Punnakayal gathered, and four or five hundred of them came with weapons down the narrow road to confront the Adi Dravidars. Many of them were drunk, having sent the catch on to the markets, and thus having finished work for the day.

Around noon, Jaiswal had received a call from the priest of the Punnakayal church saying, 'Please do something. I am not able to stop these boys. They have gathered in large numbers. They are carrying arms and they are going to Senthamangalam to settle scores. They are saying that one of the fishermen has been beaten up.'

Rumours were the biggest problem. The village folks were very gullible. If someone said to them that a crow had pecked a person's ear, and had flown away with it, the people would chase after the culprit crow even before checking if the ear on the person was still intact.

Jaiswal called the Armughaneri police station on the wireless. Someone from the police station came on the line after a while and Jaiswal asked who he was. He turned out to be the sentry on duty. The rest had gone out for some work. Jaiswal left instructions that once someone of authority, the head constable or the sub-inspector or the CHO, came to the police station, they should contact him because trouble was brewing at Punnakayal.

Jaiswal tried to contact the Siruvaikundam DSP, Pratap Singh. He had gone to Athoor for the panchayat meeting. No luck there. The priest called again, saying that the fishermen were leaving the village, hundreds of them with weapons and jerry cans filled with kerosene that was used to run their outboard engines. Jaiswal could discern the panic in his voice. Now Jaiswal himself felt apprehensive. He called the sub-inspector at Armughaneri again, but all he got was the crackle and hiss of the wireless.

Jaiswal then ran to the car, telling the five or six sentries on duty to grab their weapons, get into a jeep and follow him to Punnakayal. The Special Branch inspector and his staff were also instructed to follow in another jeep. They all set off for Punnakayal, which was forty kilometres away. Jaiswal's best hope now was to get there before the violence began. He made good progress up to Athoor. But between Athoor and Senthamangalam the road was narrow, and their progress towards Punnakayal slowed down considerably.

When Jaiswal reached Senthamangalam, the village was empty. He could see smoke rising from some thatched huts. There was one constable sitting on the side of the road where the village began. He told Jaiswal that the sub-inspector had come with two constables, all on one motorcycle. But the crowd from Punnakayal had been around six hundred in number. They attacked the village. But before they could attack Senthamangalam, the Adi Dravidars had run away, all of them – men, women, everybody. The fishermen of Punnakayal began throwing their belongings and utensils out in the open, pouring kerosene on their dwellings, setting them on fire. They even threw naatu gundu (country bombs).

Sub-Inspector Jacob and the constables tried to intervene, but it was no use. In the melee, one of the constables was injured in the head when a naatu gundu struck him and the sub-inspector had sped off on the motorcycle with the injured constable to the hospital, leaving the other to monitor the situation.

Over the silence within the empty village of Senthamangalam, Jaiswal could hear in the distance a vague, boisterous shouting from the direction of Punnakayal.

It was half past two in the afternoon. Jaiswal called for an armed reserve platoon to be sent to the location. It would take some time for them to mobilize, take their riot gear, get on to the police bus and get there. The Special Branch inspector, who was not in uniform, had set off to see if he could find out more about what had happened in Senthamangalam. Jaiswal began walking up the bund, by the side of the narrow road. The bund was thrice his height; the packed earth that rose steep had some shrubs growing in it. The soles of the regulation brown leather shoes that Jaiswal was wearing kept slipping as he leaned forward to climb the bund. Above him, clouds scuttled, kites wheeled, sea-birds passed. From the top of the bund, Jaiswal surveyed the riverbed, where water flowed in small bands. There was more vegetation, thorny shrubs grew wild, and in between acacia had grown. Gusts of wind ruffled the tall grass. Cattle egrets paced tentatively. The scenery looked incongruously peaceful and untouched by the violence on the other side of the bund.

As he gazed on the scene, Jaiswal thought he could see a man sleeping on the grass, his face towards the sky, in a posture of abandon. He called out to him, but the man didn't respond. He went down the slope and when he reached the bottom, he saw that the man had been butchered. There were cut marks all over him. On a thin gold chain, the dead man was wearing a cross.

As he turned around, he could see another body behind some acacia. When he went towards the second body, he spied yet another one – it was sunk deeper in the grass. And another and another. In all, Jaiswal counted seven dead men lying on the Thamarabarani riverbed, all with deep cuts on their bodies, some with their entrails hanging out. One of them had had his arm cut in two; it was probably a defensive injury. Jaiswal was standing in the middle of a massacre that he hadn't been able to prevent.

Strangely, all the dead men wore crosses. Evidently, they were fishermen, not Adi Dravidars. How did this happen? Five or six hundred fishermen had come to attack Senthamangalam. They had attacked. They had burnt the dwellings of the Adi Dravidars who had run away, and the fishermen had gone back to Punnakayal triumphant. Jaiswal had heard their shouts of jubilation, and yet here were seven of them butchered. Never had he seen so many killed at the same time in one place. Superintendent Anoop Jaiswal knew his troubles were just beginning.

He ran back up the bund, shouting. He told his driver, Chockalingam, the Special Branch inspector and the guards about what he had seen. All of them rushed up the bund and then down to the scene of the massacre. Jaiswal was paralysed. He ordered that nobody should talk into the wireless. There should be complete radio silence on this.

The Special Branch inspector said, 'But, sir, we have to inform someone.'

'Wait a minute', Jaiswal interrupted him. 'I need some time to think.'

He asked his driver to take his chair out of the car boot and place it beside the vehicle. Jaiswal would carry a small foldable chair, with olive green canvas seating, wherever he went. It was not something the police department had provided him; he had bought it with his own money. Jaiswal then asked for his cigarette packet – he occasionally smoked Wills Navy Cut cigarettes.

He was convinced there was going to be trouble all along the coastal road once word of the massacre spread from village to village like wildfire. Word would soon be out. The fishermen would go on a rampage. How were they not aware that their people had been murdered? How was he going to take command of the situation?

He asked the Special Branch inspector to talk to the police stations along the coastal road, like Sathankulam and Kulashekarpatnam, and instruct them to close the coastal road to all traffic.

Suddenly, Jaiswal's DIG came on the line and asked on the wireless, 'What happened, Jaiswal? Why are you closing the coastal road?' Jaiswal responded that he could not speak on the phone because there was no phone in the vicinity and he could not speak on the wireless either. He told the flabbergasted DIG that he would explain later.

Then Jaiswal told the the Tirunelveli Armed Reserve Police to mobilize their entire strength immediately and go to Athoor. His third instruction was to find all the locations of Adi Dravidar villages along the coastal road. His fourth directive was to tell the Armed Reserve Police to deploy one-tenth of their men to all the Adi Dravidar villages on the coastal road.

The DIG, meanwhile, was getting incensed by the minute on the wireless. He shouted, 'Superintendent Jaiswal, you come to the police station immediately and talk to me! Now! Immediately!'

Jaiswal told him, 'Just bear with me, sir. I will talk to you shortly. Please let me finish giving my orders.' He then drove to the nearest police station to make the phone call to the DIG. The Armughaneri police station was half an hour away. The roads were bad, and progress was slow. On the way, Jaiswal ordered that Punnakayal village be blocked.

He also gave orders for the bodies at Senthamangalam to be retrieved and sent to Tuticorin general hospital for a post-mortem after the inquest. Cases had to be registered. Muthuraj, who was at the camp office, sensed something big had happened and he got in touch with the priest of Punnakayal; all the priest knew was that Senthamangalam had been attacked and the attackers had come back to the village. Jaiswal told Muthuraj to find out how many people in the Special Branch knew or had relatives in Punnakayal and that they were to go to the village immediately and mingle among the villagers to get information.

By the time Jaiswal reached the Armughaneri police station, he had already delayed the information of the massacre for over two hours.

The first thing he did when he reached the Armughaneri police station was to call the DIG to tell him seven people had been killed. The DIG was furious.

He barked on the telephone, 'What is the reason?

'We know nothing now, sir', Jaiswal told him.

'What was the sub-inspector doing? Was he sleeping when these people were killed? Suspend the sub-inspector!' he thundered. He said he was coming from Tirunelveli to meet Jaiswal in Senthamangalam.

The collector and other authorities were informed. When Jaiswal reached Senthamangalam, the bodies had been brought up and laid side by side by the road. Ambulances had arrived. The priest had been called to identify the bodies, and word reached those in Punnakayal who had begun counting the missing. There was an uproar in the village.

The DIG arrived and a battalion of nearly seven hundred armed police were deployed from Manimuthar. A torrential downpour began without notice, and all night it rained heavily. All were thoroughly drenched. In the morning, the rain finally stopped, and the Thamarabarani was in spate. The first news that greeted Jaiswal came from a constable who had gone to relieve himself by the bund. He came shouting, 'Sir, sir, there is a body stuck in some bushes and it is going to float away.'

Jaiswal shouted, 'Pull that body to the riverbank before it floats away.' Everybody was waiting for the other to rescue the body from the river.

'Arrey!' yelled. 'Don't wait!' He began to take off his shirt to get into the water. Promptly, two constables, fully clothed, jumped into the water and pulled the body out. It was yet another body wearing a chain with a cross and it bore many injuries.

Nobody slept a wink that night. Jaiswal hadn't eaten lunch or dinner the previous day. How time had passed, he did not know. He had slept fitfully in the back seat of the Ambassador car. Soon, the DIG ordered Jaiswal to suspend the sub-inspector.

'Why, sir?' Jaiswal asked him.

'Otherwise, you will be held responsible,' he responded.

'Sir, if you are talking about moral responsibility, even the chief minister is morally responsible. The poor sub-inspector came running when he heard about the attack, and when his constable was injured in the head, he took him to hospital under the most trying circumstances – not in an ambulance, not in a jeep, but on his motorcycle. He put the constable in the front and he somehow rode to the hospital, sir. He deserves a medal, sir. I recommend him for gallantry, not for suspension, sir.'

'Don't talk back to me. He has a pistol. What is it for? Is it a showpiece?'

That day Jaiswal must have felt quite reckless. He told the DIG, 'Sir, there are only six bullets in the pistol. The fishermen were about five to six hundred in number. What could the sub-inspector have done after he had emptied his pistol? What good is a pistol when you have to confront an angry crowd like that? All three would have been lynched – Sub-Inspector Jacob and the two constables.'

Now that there was plenty of water in the river, Jaiswal bathed in it and went to relieve himself by it. Food came sometimes – somebody must have been attending to it.

Everyone had their work cut out. Jaiswal's focus was to get the sequence of events right for the report that had to be sent to the Government of Tamil Nadu. It had already been delayed, and they still didn't know what had happened, who the culprits were, how many had been arrested and how many were still at large. It was a story in progress. There were many things that needed his attention.

A trickle of information had started coming in and the story was finally pieced together. It went like this: That fateful day, on 23 November 1987, around one hundred and thirty fishermen from Punnakayal had arrived at Senthamangalam. When the Adi Dravidars saw them coming and attacking, the entire village of Senthamangalam ran away to hide. The fleeing youngsters and men carried with them whatever weapons they could find. Some of them ran to the bund and hid themselves in the shrubs and bushes growing in the riverbed.

Satisfied that they had caused enough damage to teach the inhabitants of Senthamangalam a lesson they would not soon forget, the fishermen of Punnakayal began to return to their village. Some of them, already drunk and boisterous, headed towards the river. Seeing them come over the bund, the Adi Dravidars, who had seen their homes being burnt by this very crowd, their belongings destroyed, thought they were coming to attack them.

The fishermen stood no chance; they were butchered. The noisy crowd on the other side of the high bund returning jubilantly to Punnakayal did not hear anything. All they heard was the sound of their own victory ringing in their ears. And Superintendent Jaiswal had entered the scene, like a good policeman in the movies, after all the action was over. That evening, the district collector, Mr Armugham, an elderly man, spoke to Jaiswal on the wireless.

'Helloo, helloooo,' he went feebly on the wireless. 'Mr Jaiswal, helloooo, hellooooo.'

'Sir, I am here.'

'Is it safe for me to come there?'

'Sir, I am here and so are my policemen. If it is safe for me, it must be safe for you also, sir. Please come, sir.'

The DIG, who had gone back to Tirunelveli, called Jaiswal and said he was coming as well, and with a force. The bodies needed to be handed over. The parish priest, who was trying to get everybody to gather inside the church, requested the police to bring the bodies to the building.

It was dark by the time the buses loaded with riot police reached the church. They got down from the bus and waited for instructions. Then came the bus with the bodies. It stopped about four hundred metres away from the church. Jaiswal's car drew up alongside.

From a distance, Jaiswal could already hear the women wailing. It was a strange sound – when all the women were waiting in one voice, it rose and fell like high waves. As he got out of his car, the first stones began to land on them. Like a fusillade, they kept coming. It was dark and Jaiswal did not know from where the stones were coming. He could hear the riot policemen cock their rifles. Stones hit the car and the buses. He could hear a litany of abuse rising in the air.

Jaiswal shouted to the men, 'Get into the bus, get into the bus!'

The buses were riot buses with metal grills and wire mesh on the windows instead of glass. He shouted on the inspectors, 'Get the bullets out of their chambers!' Jaiswal didn't want anybody firing. He told the inspector that no one was to fire his weapon. If any firing was to be done, Jaiswal would do it first and he would direct where to fire. As the stones began to land steadily, he ordered the drivers to keep the engine running, and instructed that no one was to get down from the bus.

The stones were coming in thick when Jaiswal ordered that the buses be turned to face the exit. Through the darkness, as he took shelter behind his car, Jaiswal saw a figure in white rushing towards him. It was the priest and he had two more people with him.

'Sir, we are calming down the village. The bodies have to be taken to the church. We will do the burial tomorrow. Tonight, the whole night, we will have prayers for the dead. Before that happens, somebody in a position of authority should come and talk to them.'

Jaiswal looked around. Muthuraj, who had arrived from Tuticorin earlier, was standing there, and so was Elavan.

'Who will go inside, sir? What if somebody stabs us in the back?' Elavan asked Jaiswal.

Jaiswal said he would go. Muthuraj was wearing a cream

shirt. Jaiswal was in uniform. He requested Muthuraj to give him his shirt.

Jaiswal began unbuttoning his uniform shirt and handed it to his driver.

Wordlessly, Muthuraj took off his bush shirt and gave it to Jaiswal to wear.

Wearing Muthuraj's shirt, Jaiswal told the priest, 'Let's go.'

Muthuraj said, 'Sir, you are forgetting your weapon.'

Jaiswal told him, 'No, Muthuraj. No weapons here. We are about to be in the presence of God.'

As they began walking towards the church, Muthuraj followed behind, in his banian. Jaiswal hissed loudly at him, 'Put on a shirt, put on a shirt! You cannot enter the church looking like that!' But he wouldn't listen. The priest took Jaiswal into the building from the back; they had to walk the long aisle all the way to the pulpit while the crowd on both sides of the aisle shouted and the women wailed.

The priest spoke over their shouting for more than twenty minutes before there was some semblance of order. All the time as he calmed the crowd down, Jaiswal kept thinking about what he could tell this crowd of angry people in his pathetic Tamil. He feared his Tamil – or lack of it – would make matters worse. He would undoubtedly fumble.

When face to face with the gathered mass, he told them that the biggest issue in his mind was that someone had been at fault here and that was why they were all here in the church, in the house of God. Jaiswal said that he had been thinking about it for two days and he had an answer.

Jaiswal finally told them, 'It was my fault that these innocent people died. Somewhere I committed a mistake, a mistake worse than any sin you could think of.' He continued, 'What that mistake is, I have no idea. But I am searching for answers and God will help me find it just as how God has showed me that I am to blame. I am to blame because it is my duty to protect you. You, and all others in the district, I failed. I cannot blame anyone else. If there is another body that has to fall, it has to be mine, and no one else's.'

To his surprise the crowd fell silent. The handover of the bodies began, the wailing rose and fell, rose and fell, rose and fell, like some liturgy. It was past midnight when Chockalingam, Jaiswal's driver, brought his car around and Jaiswal left. He told Chockalingam, 'Nalla passi iruku.' (I am feeling very hungry.) 'Yengey saapaad kadaikkum? Athoorley?' (Where can we get some food? In Athoor?)

But all shops were closed at that time of the night.

Chockalingam said, 'Illai aiyyah, amma periya dabbah anupitanga.' (No, sir, madam has sent a big tiffin carrier for you.)

Constables in the camp office had told Neelam the gist of what they had been hearing on the wireless and she had cooked chicken and rice, packed a lot of it, and through the camp office motorcycle used for carrying thapal (postal) messages, sent it to Chockalingam, so that Jaiswal could eat. Jaiswal told Chockalingam to pull the car over to the side of the road and get his chair out.

'What about you?' Jaiswal asked Chockalingam. The tiffin carrier was filled with food.

Chockalingam said, 'Sir, I will find food somewhere.'

'No, there is enough for both. Do you like chicken?'

Chockalingam sat on the driver's seat, Jaiswal sat on the chair. With the car door open and the church lights glowing faintly far behind them, the two ate the best meal of their lives, sitting on the side of the dark road. All around them, fireflies flitted about, frogs croaked in premonition of the hard rain that was about to fall.

That would have been a good place to end this story. But that is not what happened. For a month, the deployment remained in place. Jaiswal was called upon to explain why there had been a delay in conveying information about the massacre. An enquiry began so as to eke out the lapses in the investigation.

Jaiswal responded that his first instinct had been to prevent the situation from escalating. If he had spoken on the wireless, the news of the massacre would have spread to everyone. He had wanted to ensure that he deployed his forces before he let the news out. It was in the interest of law and order that he hadn't informed on the wireless, and given the circumstances, there had been no other way of conveying the details. In the course of the enquiry, the priest told the DGP that he had called the SP. The DGP looked up the exchange records to find out at what time the priest had called Jaiswal, what time the SP arrived and who were the people who had accompanied the SP.

The DGP came to see Jaiswal after fifteen days and Jaiswal received him at Tirunelveli at the India Cements guest house, on the outskirts of the city. They had breakfast together. The DIG was also there, as was the inspector general (IG) of Madurai. They left for Punnakayal village. Not once did the DGP ask Jaiswal what the situation was.

At the church, the priest was waiting, and the village elders along with a big crowd of villagers were also present. The DG told Jaiswal to wait while he and the DIG went into the building. They were inside for nearly two hours. Jaiswal sat on a chair under a mango tree. Then the DGP came, and said, 'Jaiswal, okay, fine. Things are quiet. Keep a watch on things.'

Then as he turned to the car, he pointed to a woman who was standing in the crowd that had come out of the church and said, 'Jaiswal, that woman has saved you.'

Jaiswal could not recognize her. He asked, 'In what way, sir?'

DGP Ravindran told him that the woman spoke for the entire village. She had said that the police were not to be trusted, but the one who had come with the red light flashing in the car was doing good work. The DGP asked her who this person was. The people told him it was the SP.

I could end the story here, but I would like to add a coda.

Sub-Inspector Jacob would retire later as an inspector. In 2012, Jaiswal was the chairman of the Police Housing Corporation. He had become the director general of police. He was sitting in his office when an army officer, a lieutenant colonel, came to his office. He introduced himself as the son-in-law of Inspector Jacob. The DGP asked how Jacob was doing. He told Jaiswal that Jacob had suffered a massive heart attack. He was in the ICU in Billroth Hospital, in Kilpauk, which was nearby, after a bypass surgery. That morning the son-in-law had spoken to Inspector Jacob, who had told him that while he was in Chennai if he could meet or talk to Jaiswal, he would be very happy.

DGP Jaiswal immediately stood up and both rushed to see Jacob at Billroth. The hospital staff permitted them into the ICU, and there lay Jacob, with tubes attached to his body.

Seeing Jaiswal, Jacob smiled.

'You are going to be okay, Jacob. Don't worry,' Jaiswal assured him.

Jacob kept smiling.

'I wanted to see you,' he said.

'Was it twenty years ago that I last saw you?'

'Yes, sir. I become an inspector, thanks to you.'

'Don't thank me, Jacob. Thank God. I had nothing to do with it!'

He couldn't talk much and Jaiswal sat for a few minutes and then left. Two hours later, his son-in-law called to say Inspector Jacob had passed away.

9

A Mistake of Fact

Those days, if you were a girl below sixteen years of age, you were a minor. The girl in question was about four or five months shy of legally being allowed to decide whom she could marry. Her parents, fieldworkers and labourers, came to the Maniachi police station and complained that their minor daughter had eloped with a man who worked as a conductor in the Kattaboman Transport Corporation.

Along with the mother and father, the local zamindar had sent some of his people to ensure that the case was registered with due care. The zamindar had also contacted the range DIG who ordered that a special party be formed to recover the girl from the clutches of the conductor as quickly as possible, before it was too late. A case of kidnapping was registered, and the investigation began.

The police party went to the house of the accused, where she had last been seen, and began to make enquiries by speaking to her friends. Luck did not favour them, though; they were not able to trace the couple that day.

Jaiswal was in the camp office the next morning when a couple walked into his room. The man was fairly tall and wore a spotless white shirt, while the woman – more a girl than a woman – wore a saree that looked stiff, shiny and new.

The man did all the talking. He said the two had married the previous day and now they had come to surrender. When Jaiswal asked them where they had come from, they said they were from Maniachi. Jaiswal asked the girl what her age was, and she told him.

'You could have waited for four or five months, couldn't you? What was the hurry? You have committed a very serious offence. How old are you?' asked Jaiswal of the man.

'Twenty-four, sir,' he said.

'That's old enough to know right from wrong. I don't think I can do anything for you.'

Yet, it seemed odd to Jaiswal that the man, a bus conductor, who had a good job and the prospects of pension, should risk his all by running away with a minor girl. It also seemed odd that the parents of the girl, labourers, should object to the girl marrying someone above their economic stature, who could look after their daughter and provide for her.

He called for her parents to come to the camp office, to see if there could be a way to prevent criminal action being taken; if there was some way for a compromise. After all, this was a love story. He also called the investigating officer in the kidnapping case, an inspector.

In about three hours, the parents arrived in a small van, and as soon as they saw their daughter, the mother went screaming towards her, saying she had ruined them, and the girl cowered behind her new husband while the father meekly stood by, watching. Their other children, a young son and a younger daughter, had also come along. The little girl looked lost and the boy, frightened. The brother kept his hand continuously on his sister's shoulder as if to reassure her.

The inspector intervened and said this was a police station and therefore proper decorum was to be maintained. If the mother kept shouting, she would be locked up for her unruly behaviour, along with the rest of them. But the mother was adamant. 'I want my daughter back,' she kept shouting. 'I will not accept this marriage.'

The father kept quiet and Jaiswal was not able to make out whether it was because she didn't allow him to speak, or whether she spoke for the both of them. Jaiswal asked the mother and the father to approach the table where he was sitting and instructed the inspector to take the children outside while he talked to the parents. Once outside, the inspector had tea and biscuits brought for the children so as to calm them. He then tried to find out from them what had really happened.

What the younger brother told the inspector was startling. He rushed to the Special Branch on the first floor and called Jaiswal on the phone – the story was not a love story after all; it was something else altogether. The mother has sold the girl, he informed the SP.

'What are you saying?' Jaiswal said into the phone. The

inspector apprised him of the actual situation: The mother had sold the girl to the zamindar, so that his cousin, a thatha (a grandfather) of about sixty years of age and who had become a widower recently, could marry her.

The girl had been sold for Rs 25,000. The zamindar had given the mother half the amount as advance and the woman had taken it. The remaining was to be given as soon as the girl married the old man. The boy, the girl's brother, claimed that the van the woman and the family had come in had been sent by the zamindar.

The girl had not wanted to be married to the old man, but the mother kept pressuring her. The boy said that when his sister left home, the zamindar wanted his money back but his mother and father had already spent the money and did not know how to return it. The mother had assured the zamindar, who had come raging to their home, that she would get the girl back and the marriage would go ahead as planned.

In English, Jaiswal instructed that the inspector should take down the boy's statement verbatim right there, while the mother and the father remained with him. When the boy's statement had been registered, Jaiswal sent the mother away, and confronted the father separately with the statement. The father did not deny it. At one point, he seemed to even accept it by asking, 'What do you want us to do? We are very poor and we have many debts.'

Jaiswal could make out that the father was softer on the daughter than his wife, who kept blaming the daughter for their plight. Poverty was so crushing that they were helpless. The father seemed to suggest that the zamindar was powerful and he had put a value on his daughter, a far greater value than they, as parents, could think of. Jaiswal tried to absorb what the father had just said. For him, that the father did not deny the explanation became a corroboration of evidence provided by the son.

The investigating officer pointed out that a case of kidnapping had already been registered. Jaiswal thought for a while, and said to the inspector, 'What is kidnapping? It means moving a minor away from the custody of a guardian, against his or her will, without permission or by force for an illegal purpose.'

He called for the dictionary. There was one in the residence, the Oxford English Dictionary. He asked for it to be brought to him and looked up the word 'guardian'. A guardian was someone who cared for and protected the interests of someone, usually a minor, who was incapable of looking after himself or herself and his or her interests.

Jaiswal asked the investigating officer a rhetorical question: On the day the parents decided to sell their daughter to an old man for a sum of Rs 25,000, mainly to repay their debts, had they not forfeited, in full plain view, the right to be the guardians who were in charge of the welfare of their ward?

They had placed their own interests above those of their ward. And if they were no guardians, what did it make the girl? It made her an orphan. By giving shelter and protection to the orphan, and by ensuring her well-being, the conductor had committed no crime.

The inspector said, 'What you are saying may be generally true, sir, but you are making an absurd argument. It is not going to work.'

Jaiswal told him, 'I know you are scared of the repercussions. But I am convinced.' He called the camp clerk, Velayudham, and instructed that the enquiry was to be conducted at the camp office because the couple had surrendered there, and so the investigating officer had to go there.

Their statements were recorded, and from the statements it appeared as follows: the parents had sold the girl for a consideration of Rs 25,000, and having taken an advance, they were not able to repay the amount because the girl had eloped. Hence, they were under duress. By any stretch of the imagination, they were not guardians, and the girl had run away, fearing the worst fate that could befall her if she was handed over to the person who had bought her. Hence, in the opinion of the superintendent of police, it was a question of 'mistake of fact', and there was no kidnapping as had been made out.

Jaiswal told the investigating officer that the burden of proof was now entirely on himself, and he would take the blame if needed. The inspector was satisfied, and he went ahead and closed the case.

Jaiswal told the girl to go back to her parents, and she would have protection from the police, as would the boy. There was no case now. After five months, she would be free to do what she wanted. Jaiswal sent word through the parents that if the zamindar threatened them again, a criminal case would be registered against him. Handing over money to buy a minor girl was offence enough.

The zamindar moved the Madras High Court, saying the superintendent of police had interfered in the case, wrongfully, and the high court issued a notice to Jaiswal for personal appearance.

The case was referred as a 'mistake of fact'. Jaiswal travelled from Tuticorin to Madras and met his DGP who laughed heartily, saying, 'You are not a first-time offender, Jaiswal. What is it with you and the courts? It's always some court, the Supreme Court or the high court.'

Jaiswal tried to explain the situation to him and he said, 'No, this is between you and the courts. Explain it there. I want no part of this.'

At the high court hearing, the judge looked at him and said, 'Mr SP, in future, please leave such interpretations to the court. Do you understand?'

'Milord,' Jaiswal responded, 'I could have done that. But it would have been too late and imagine what irreparable damage it would have caused to the two innocent lives. As an SP, I had to take a decision then and there. There was no malice in my action.'

The judge allowed himself a small smile. He took off his spectacles and twirled them thoughtfully, saying, 'Anyway, we accept your explanation in this case and we caution you to be more careful in the future. Case dismissed.'

10

The Weakling

The guard saluted Superintendent Anoop Jaiswal as he stepped outside his residence, saying, 'Sir, there is a man who is loitering outside. He seems to be coming here and going away. He has been doing that since six in the morning.'

It was seven thirty now. Jaiswal had not changed into his uniform yet.

'If he wants to meet me, call him,' he said and went to the camp office a few steps away. The guard opened the main gate and went outside to see if the man was still there.

The newspapers had arrived and were arranged on the desk and Jaiswal began reading them. Shortly afterwards, the guard came and told him the man was waiting to see him. A man came into the room, puny and very thin. He couldn't have been more than twenty-six years old. He had a very frightened expression on his face and he came carrying a thick cloth bag. He was holding it at his side and his hands were shaking.

'Please tell me how I can help you,' Jaiswal prompted him. He could see that the man wanted to speak but was unable to. Some sounds came out, but he could not decipher what he was saying.

'Speak loudly,' Jaiswal urged him, thinking maybe he was speech impaired. He instructed water to be given to the man. When it came, the man took the tumbler of water, but his hand was trembling when he put it to his mouth to drink, and water spilled down his shirt.

'Please sit down, if you don't tell me what you want, I will not be able to help you.'

He kept standing and again tried to say something but he simply couldn't. He was agitated now, and suddenly he took a couple of steps and stood next to Jaiswal and opened the mouth of the bag. As he opened it, he managed to stutter, 'Aiyyah, oru sinna thappu ayi poitathu' (Sir, I have committed a small blunder). He pushed the bag with the partly open mouth towards Jaiswal.

Jaiswal looked inside. Then he cried out, aghast, 'What is this?'

Inside was a bloody mess of what appeared to be a very large, severed human head, that of a male with a mass of hair lying on its side. The man's hands kept shivering, and the bag kept shaking. Jaiswal immediately took the bag, placed it on the ground by the table and took the man outside and made him sit. He ordered the guard to keep an eye on him, came back into his office room and called the Tuticorin South Police Station.

It was shortly after the morning roll call in the police station and everyone was present. He asked the inspector to come immediately to the camp office. He also called for Mr Vadivel, the Special Branch inspector. Then he went home and changed into his uniform.

The Tuticorin South Police Station inspector came within fifteen or twenty minutes. When he came back, Jaiswal requested the inspector to ask the man who had brought the head what his story was. Jaiswal could see flies had begun to buzz around the bag, but the man kept sitting still, unmindful of the flies that settled on him, though occasionally he shook a little, involuntarily.

The man who brought the head to the camp office lived in a village in the Ambasamudram subdivision. A labourer, dirt poor, he lived with his mother and young wife whom he had recently married. His sister lived in a neighbouring village, and that fateful day his mother had gone visiting his sister. His marriage had been arranged by his sister, and initially he had resisted, but they insisted and he gave in after many months. After their marriage, the man grew fond of his wife and the initial hesitations fell away. He continued to find work as a labourer in the fields.

There was no toilet in the hut where they lived. They had to go out into the fields to answer nature's call, taking a chombu (a small metal pot filled with water) to clean up afterwards. His wife usually went out for this purpose before the sun rose and many times, she had felt that someone was following her into the fields. For weeks, this feeling of being followed persisted, and she was sure that someone was watching her as she relieved herself. She told her husband about it and he started to accompany her and waited till she finished. Then, one day, he had to leave for work early and she went alone. This time she spotted the person, only an outline, but she was sure it was their neighbour.

Their neighbour was a large man, stronger and bigger than her husband, and it was said he was well to do. He lived in a house a stone's throw away, further down the road, and it was a concrete house with many rooms, painted pink and with green wooden windows. A water tap stood guard outside at the back of the house and it had a granite stone ledge on which clothes were washed. There was a toilet and a bathroom that stood alone at the back of the house, a half-moon cut into the wall high up, functioning as a window. There was no need for the neighbour to answer the call of nature out in the open field. That day, when her husband came back from work she told him of her suspicions. He went and asked the neighbour to stop following his wife into the fields. The neighbour shouted him down, denied doing it and dismissed him.

When it happened again, he complained to the people in the village. The village elders questioned the neighbour, and the man laughed it away and that was the end of the matter. But it was out in the open now.

The neighbour accosted the man and said, 'Oh, you have become bold enough to complain to the village? Look what happened. They did not believe you. Now, I will come and enjoy your wife in your own house. Just you wait and see.'

This sent chills through him, and he went into shock. For the next few days, he stopped going to work, and accompanied his wife everywhere she went, even stood guard as she sprinkled water outside their hut and drew a kolam in the morning or swept the ground clean. From a distance, the neighbour watched him with a taunting smile.

One day, as he and his wife stepped out, the neighbour called out, 'How long are you going to guard her like this? And what makes you think you are strong enough to be a guard? Do you really think you can fight me off?'

After hearing this, he couldn't sleep. He didn't go to work. He thought of sending his wife to her mother's house. But for how long? They were dirt poor and he couldn't afford to go without work indefinitely. For days together, the only food they ate was pazhaya soru (leftover rice soaked in water overnight till it became fermented). This was mashed, and thin butter milk along with pieces of green chilli and at times onion was added

That was their meal, day after day, sometimes the only meal.

Early one morning, he saw his neighbour who started taunting him again, 'Yennada innam kaavalkaran velai panrayaa? Yevalo nalikku than nee pannuvai? Oru naal aval yen kayyil varuval, ni paathute irrupai!' (Still playing the guard? Let me see for how long. One day, she will be with me, and you will be left watching.)

The neighbour opened the tap and bent down to let water flow on to his head and face. Seizing the opportunity, the man went back into his hut, picked up an aruval, tiptoed past his sleeping wife, crept up on the neighbour and hacked his neck. The neighbour either hadn't seen him coming or it had never crossed his mind that the puny man would have the courage to do something like that.

On the third blow, the head fell like a coconut and rolled a little distance, eyes still open in surprise. The man picked up the head by the wet hair, and ran and ran and ran, blood dripping from the severed head. He ran till he reached the next village and there, for some reason, he hid the head and confessed to someone who was a small-time lawyer. The lawyer asked the man where the head was. He demanded to be taken there, and both went there with a cloth bag. He asked the man to put the head in the bag and take it straight to the superintendent of police in Tuticorin and surrender. That was how the man had come to the camp office.

Jaiswal had no way of knowing if he was telling the truth. But the fact that he had come with the head showed that it was not a pre-planned murder. Murderers usually tried to hide their crime. This man hadn't. He carried the evidence all the way to the camp office by bus from Ambasamudram.

Jaiswal asked that the man be taken to the South Police Station, so he could surrender. The murder had not happened in his jurisdiction. He, therefore, gave instructions to the effect that the man's statement be recorded verbatim, his motive, events leading to the recovery of the head, and the circumstances.

A wireless message was sent to the police station that

covered his village. Soon a team came and took the head for post-mortem, while another went to look for the rest of the body. Though the murder had been reported to the police station, nobody was sure what had happened. The villagers had seen the headless body and reported it to the police station. In that village, even in their wildest imagination, they had never thought that this weakling could do such a thing as murder. He hadn't told his wife, either. She was worried that he had disappeared without telling her. That had never happened before.

The man was charged with culpable homicide, not amounting to murder. He had faced constant taunts, threats and provocations from his neighbour. The village elders had failed to offer remedy or even take cognizance. The circumstances leading to the murder, taken together, amounted to grave provocation. It had, finally, broken him and he lost his self-control under the crushing weight of the knowledge that his wife would not be safe as long as the neighbour had his eyes on her. The sentence based on all this meant that after a few years he could be free and go back to his wife.

11

Case and Counter-case

In the Tuticorin rural subdivision falls a village called Mudathur. There was no police station in that village. From Mudathur, people had come to the town's South Police Station to submit a complaint. That was how a complaint was filed against Thalamuthu, who had attacked someone with an aruval. A case under Section 307 was registered, which was attempt to murder. A few days later, the same people were back again. Thalamuthu had come back with his aruval and tried to kill someone else.

Thalamuthu was not from the caste which was the local majority. The people from Mudathur said that since Thalamuthu was prowling around with an aruval, if he was not arrested soon, he could get lucky and kill someone again. The DIG B.P. Nailwal was aware of this case. Maybe they had petitioned him directly, or maybe someone knew him.

Jaiswal was a newcomer. He was aware of what was going on, but it was all happening behind his back. On the orders of the DIG, the very next day, the second case was registered. A team of police officers was formed, led by DSP Rural, whose name was Chockalingam. Chockalingam was a young DSP. This was his first posting and he would go on to rise all the way to retire as an IG.

The job of Chockalingam and his team was to nab Thalamuthu. No other work was given to them. For about a week or ten days, all they had to do was concentrate on nabbing Thalamuthu before he could use his aruval again to attack somebody.

Since Jaiswal kept an open house, and had visitors coming all through the day, word got around that the superintendent lent a patient ear. He often did not know if the people who came to meet him were telling the truth, or at least the partial truth, and if so, which part was untrue. It was tiring sometimes.

He had a standard response. Whenever anyone came to see him with a complaint, the first question he asked was 'Have you been to the local police station? Have you made a complaint there?' Often the answer would be 'No'. Often people did not register a complaint at the local police station because they felt they would not be heard, there. So, Jaiswal would pick up the wireless and call the senior officer of the police station that the complainant should have visited and say, 'I am sending such and such a person with a complaint. Kindly receive the complaint and look into it at the earliest. Kindly send me a small reply on the action taken by you once you have attended to the complaint.'

At this turn of events, the visitor would normally be crestfallen. Here was the person who had come all the way from his faraway village to file a complaint, and the SP was sending him to the local police station. Seeing the dejected looks, Jaiswal would tell the visitor, 'Please go to the police station and I assure you action will be taken. If you are not satisfied with the result, please come back to me, and I will personally attend to it.' Usually, the police station was flooded with complaints and the visitor would eventually go back to the SP stating that the complaint was not looked into. It was never in the interest of the police station for the petitioner to go back to the SP to say he had been left unattended or given less than a fair hearing.

Sometimes Jaiswal would ask the specific inspector when he could attend to the problem. The inspector would generally ask for two or three days' time. Naturally, it is not possible for a policeman to attend to every complaint the minute it is received. Jaiswal would then give ten days to a fortnight to take action. He would tell the inspector to intimate the same time frame to the complainant, even if he was able to deal with it in a couple of days. If you told the complainant that you would look into it in two days and were, for some reason, unable to do so for, let's say four days, the complainant would begin to lose hope, again. The uncertainty of the wait put a great burden on the mind. The wait would seem longer than it really was.

One night Jaiswal had finished with seeing visitors or so he thought. As he readied to go home, he had a visitor. The person came into the room but would not sit. He stood with his arms crossed across his chest. He looked as if he was in his early thirties. Although Jaiswal invited him to sit, he kept standing and said, 'I am Thalamuthu.'

'Okay, Thalamuthu, sit down, and tell me what have you come for.'

He kept standing. 'I am Mudathur Thalamuthu,' he repeated.

'Oh ho. So, you are the Mudathur Thalamuthu, the famous Thalamuthu, whom the police is searching everywhere for. I must say you hide very well. Where have you been hiding?'

'They are taking action against me, but what are they doing about the other party? They tried to molest my sister, not once but twice, and what action was taken against them? Nothing.'

'Thalamuthu, I don't know about it. You can give the complaint about it even now. But you know very well that won't absolve you of your action.'

Muthuraj, from the Special Branch, was still there in the office. Jaiswal called him in and told him to write down the complaint Thalamuthu was giving. Jaiswal would forward it to the Mudathur inspector to look into it and, if necessary, a case would be registered.

'We will be taking action, Thalamuthu,' Jaiswal told him after his complaint had been registered.

Thalamuthu then said, 'You can arrest me now,' and held out his hands.

It was not unusual for people who came to the camp office to surrender. Neelam was witness to one such surrender. Someone had come to the camp office asking to see the SP, and the guards allowed him and he was sitting on the floor. Jaiswal had gone to Tirunelveli, and was delayed there. When the visitor went upstairs to the Special Branch office, no one noticed. Thangavelu, the inspector from Muthiahpuram walked into the camp office and asked the guards if someone with of such and such name had come there. The guard told him that one such person had gone upstairs. So Thangavelu ran upstairs and caught hold of that person who had come to see Jaiswal and began to push him down the stairs. The person began to shout and argue with the inspector. Hearing the noise of the quarrel, Neelam came out. She saw the inspector holding the man by his collar. The guard told her that the inspector had come to arrest the man and he was resisting.

'What for? Why has he come here then?'

The man shouted that before his arrest he wanted to meet the SP aiyyah.

Neelam looked at the inspector and told him, 'Let him be here. The SP will be here soon. After he meets the SP, you can arrest him.'

Thangavelu told Neelam, 'Madam, he is a dangerous fellow.'

'So, tie him up while you wait,' Neelam told Inspector Thangavelu.

The guard then told the inspector, 'Naan guard roomle ukkara vechudarein. SP ippo varanga.' (I will keep him confined in the guard room. The SP will be here soon.)

After Neelam had gone, the inspector threatened the guard, but the guard stood firm.

It turned out to be a case of robbery and connivance. The man had stolen money and the inspector promised the man that if he led the inspector to the loot, he would set him free. The man took the inspector to the spot where the money was hidden. The inspector showed a small portion of the loot as having been recovered and kept most of the stolen money for himself. The inspector had let the thief remain at large for a couple of days, but now he wanted to book him for the theft. The inspector had betrayed the thief. Now the inspector made a counterclaim that the thief was making the allegation only because he was being arrested. It was the word of one against the other. Jaiswal ordered that a CID enquiry be conducted into it. Trust could be easily misplaced.

Coming back to Thalamuthu's case, Jaiswal didn't know what came over him, but he told Thalamuthu, 'This is my house, Thalamuthu. I don't arrest people here. You do one thing. You go to the Town South police station and surrender or go to the court and surrender. It is up to you.'

Thalamuthu thought about it and then said he would go to the court the next day and surrender. Jaiswal responded he would forward Thalamuthu's complaint and endorsed it in front of him. Thalamuthu went away. Muthuraj watched Thalamuthu leave and didn't say anything.

It must have been out of some sense of mischief that Jaiswal called Chockalingam, the rural DSP who was entrusted with the duty of arresting Thalamuthu, on the phone and asked him, 'Chockalingam, what has happened in the Thalamuthu matter? Have you been able to locate him?'

'Sir, we have come to know that he is hiding in the big banana grove in the periya vazhaithottam outside Mudathur village. We are going to raid the place at night. All preparations have been made.'

'Stop bluffing, Chockalingam. This fellow Thalamuthu came and met me and he will surrender tomorrow.'

'Sir, what do you mean he will surrender tomorrow? You let him go, sir? But you should not have allowed him to leave. He is a very bad fellow.'

'Chockalingam, he came of his own accord. I didn't call him. He said he will surrender tomorrow.'

Until evening the following day, there was no sign of Thalamuthu, neither at the police station nor at the court. Somehow this news reached the DIG and Chockalingam told him that Mudathur Thalamuthu had visited the SP's office and the SP had let him go. When Thalamuthu failed to surrender the DIG called Jaiswal and was livid.

'What is this, Jaiswal? What are you up to? What if he commits another crime? What if he kills someone else? Who will be responsible? What answer will you give? You are taking the matter very lightly, Jaiswal. Don't do it again.'

Jaiswal felt a little low after the call. Perhaps the DIG was right. The anxiety only increased when days passed and still there was no sign of either Thalamuthu surrendering or of Chockalingam getting his act together to nab Thalamuthu.

Later that week, DSP Chockalingam was sitting with Jaiswal in the office and who walked in – none other than Thalamuthu. Jaiswal saw him and called him in immediately. 'Vanga, vanga, vanga, Maapplai!' (Come in, come in, son-in-law of the house!)

Then Jaiswal asked Chockalingam, 'Ivar yaar theriyuma?' (Do you know who this gentleman is?)

The DSP could not recognize him since he had never seen him.

Then, Jaiswal looked at Thalamuthu and told him, 'You have caused me a lot of trouble. You nearly made me lose my job. You promised to surrender, but you did not.'

He pointed to Chockalingam and said, 'This police officer and his whole special team have been looking for you, and I let you go because you promised you would surrender and I trusted you.'

Chockalingam immediately stood up and said, 'Thalamuthu?' and was about to arrest him. Jaiswal told Chockalingam, 'Please sit. I want to hear what Thalamuthu has to say.'

'Sir, this fellow is a dangerous person. Why are you being so lenient?'

Thalamuthu said, 'Illai, saar.' (No, sir.) 'There are two or three cases against me, and when I left your office after promising that I would surrender, I realized that if I surrendered, I wouldn't get bail easily, and there were certain family matters that I had to settle before I surrendered. This was the reason for the delay. Please forgive me. That is what

I have come to tell you. I am not absconding. I will surrender tomorrow in the court.'

The DSP was agitated. 'No, sir. Don't let him go this time.'

Something came over Jaiswal. He ordered Chockalingam, 'You sit down. Be calm. You are not able to catch this man, you and your entire team. Yet again and again, Thalamuthu is walking freely in and out of my office. I can see how hard you have worked for his arrest. Now you deserve a break. Take it easy, now. Relax. Have a little trust.'

Then turning to Thalamuthu, Jaiswal told him, 'I cannot hold my DSP in my office for more than half an hour.'

'Illai, aiyyah, naliaikku panneerarein.' (I will do it tomorrow, sir.) Thalamuthu briefly stood with folded hands, then he vanished.

The next day, Thalamuthu surrendered in the court. He was in jail for some time. While in jail, he sent word through a constable that his sister was ill and he wanted help to have her admitted to a hospital. He said he would repay whatever the expenses were. Could Jaiswal help?

Jaiswal had his sister taken to Rajam Nursing Home, the same hospital where Antony Mookkan's wife had been treated. It was appendicitis or something. When he came out on bail, Thalamuthu went to meet Jaiswal and also went to thank Dr Ravindran for having looked after his sister. Dr Ravindran hadn't charged him. Jaiswal did not know what transpired between Thalamuthu and Dr Ravindran, but Thalamuthu started working in the clinic as a helper.

He worked there for three or four years while the case was ongoing. Afterwards, with the money he had been able to save, Thalamuthu had left for Thiruchendur where he opened a coffee shop. I am told his coffee was quite good.

12

Gratitude

One day, Jaiswal's daughter, Mini, who was then four years old, stood at the camp office door with a piece of paper. She wore a serious expression on her face.

When he saw her at the door, Jaiswal asked her, 'Yenna amma, yenna venum?' (Yes, ma'am. What do you want?')

Mini solemnly held out the piece of paper and said it was a petition, which she wanted to give him. Jaiswal told her, 'Okay, give the petition to me and I will look into it.'

Mini ran into the room and handed her father the folded piece of paper. He opened it and saw it was blank. He asked her, 'Yenna amma, yenna achchu?' (What happened?)

Mini spoke better Tamil than him, and he was happy to play along. 'Superintendent sir, yenodu appa veetukkey vara maataru. neenga avarai devaseithu veetukku annupungo.' (Superintendent sir, my father never comes home. Can you please send him home?)

The others in the room were smiling. Jaiswal had no choice but to excuse himself.

As Mini led him by her little hand home for dinner, he knew that Neelam must have put Mini up to it. He had so many visitors that often he could not spend time with his children when they had a holiday, or help them fly a kite, or go for a drive, or even for an occasional swim. He maintained a running register in the camp office to keep track of all the complaints that he received. Each complaint was numbered, and the camp clerk was in charge of monitoring the progress. Three constables helped him track each of the complaints through constant calls to the police stations where the cases were registered and to get updates on the status of the complaints.

This story is one that didn't get registered. When he came back the next day, one of his visitors was a middle-aged woman in her late fifties, a widow who lived alone. Sub-Inspector Muthuraj from Special Branch was with Jaiswal when she came into the office room. She told them she had come from a village in Sathankulam, nearly fifty kilometres away. She had a son who had gone to work in some company in Kakinada, in Andhra Pradesh, about a year ago. He was her only child. He sent money to her regularly and every fortnight he wrote letters to his mother. She would also write letters to him. In the last two months, she had received no letters from her son, not even one, and no money either. Now, she couldn't sleep at night worrying about her son.

This wasn't a police matter, and Jaiswal told her, 'Amma, often children become busy with other things or they might have spent the money on something else. Sometimes they forget to write.' He advised her to have patience and told her to wait, and that her son would soon write to her. He urged her to write to her son again.

'No, sir. My son is not like that. I know him. He will never neglect me like this. I am getting terrible nightmares now. All I want to know is that my son is well and I don't know how to find out. Please help me.'

Jaiswal didn't know what to do. Kakinada was in another state.

'Sir, we can talk to the Kakinada SP,' Muthuraj suggested, to find out about this person's whereabouts.

Jaiswal looked at him and asked, 'Do you know the phone number of the Kakinada SP, or his name?'

'No, sir, I don't. But we can connect to the telephone exchange and find out the STD code for Kakinada and request to get the telephone number of the Kakinada SP.'

Jaiswal was a bit exasperated as there were so many other things that he had to attend to, but he told Muthuraj, 'Okay, you find out.' They took down the name of her son and the company he worked for and in what capacity, and asked the lady to wait outside. In less than an hour, Muthuraj was back with the Kakinada SP's office telephone number. Seeing Muthuraj come back, the woman who had been waiting outside, followed him in.

Jaiswal rang the Kakinada number and to his good fortune the Kakinada SP was in the office. He introduced himself as SP from Tuticorin in Tamil Nadu and the Kakinda SP's response was very encouraging.

Jaiswal told him, 'Sir, it is nothing much. But there is a woman waiting for her son who is working in Kakinada. I was just calling to know if everything was all right with the son, as the mother hadn't heard from him for two months.'

He gave him the details of the woman's story, the name of her son, the company he was working for and the address of the company. He also gave him the camp office number. The PA of the Kakinada SP took down the details. The Kakinada SP said, 'Okay, Jaiswal. I will find out and call your office when I have the information.'

After Jaiswal put the receiver down, he told the woman that they had asked for the information and when it arrived, someone from the Sathankulam police station would convey the information to her. He told her to go home and wait. She nodded and left.

In the evening, Muthuraj told him that the woman had not gone, and was waiting, instead. Jaiswal asked him where she was waiting. In the bus stand opposite the camp office, Muthuraj had bought some idlis and had them sent to her.

The next morning, Jaiswal had to go for a parade at Tirunelveli, and it was to start at seven. He had to leave before six to be on time. As he walked to the car to leave, he saw the woman still sitting at the bus stand. When she saw the SP, she stood up and folded her hands.

Jaiswal waved to her and gestured that she should sit down and wait. He finished the parade, met the DIG and left for Tirunelveli. It must have been around noon by then. There was no time now to go to the district police office, which was in Tuticorin town. Jaiswal asked the driver to go straight to the camp office.

As the car was entering his residence compound, Jaiswal saw that the woman was still sitting. The moment she saw him, she stood up. Muthuraj was in the office and Jaiswal asked him, as he wiped his shoes on the door mat, if there was any news from Kakinada.

Muthuraj said gravely, 'There is news. Please come in and I will tell you.' Muthuraj told him that an inspector had called from Kakinada. About thirty-five days ago, the woman's son was brought to a hospital. He was gravely ill. He was admitted in the hospital and died after a few days.

'Any foul play?'

'No, sir. No foul play.'

'Have you told her?'

'No, sir. I don't have the courage to tell her.'

'Either way, we have to tell her.'

'Yes, sir, but I can't do it.'

'But, before telling her, we have to be doubly sure.'

'Yes, sir.'

Jaiswal picked up the phone and again rang up the SP of Kakinada. He was in the office, and when he learnt the SP from Tuticorin was on the line, he asked, 'Didn't our inspector inform your office?'

'He did inform. I just wanted to cross-check.'

'I verified it,' the SP said. He gave the dates, the details, and said there was no hanky-panky. Jaiswal thanked him and put the phone down. He asked Muthuraj to bring the woman into the office. Jaiswal could see the trepidation on her hands and face and in the way she walked when she came in. He was still trying to frame sentences or words to convey the news to her. He, too, didn't know how to tell her.

She came in and saw the expression on the SP's face, saw him struggling to say something and emitted a loud scream and collapsed to the ground. They splashed some water on her face to revive her, and Jaiswal tasked the camp office jeep driver, Kanakaraj, to take her to a nearby nursing home. They took her there, and she was put on saline drip. In the evening, Muthuraj told the SP that she had recovered enough to sit up, but she was in shock and wasn't able to speak. The next day she seemed more aware of her surroundings and Jaiswal instructed that the camp office jeep take her back to her village. There, he hoped her relatives or friends would take care of her. There was nothing more that could be done.

Two months passed. Jaiswal was sitting in the main office, the district police office, when he saw the woman walking into his room. He got up from his chair and she straightaway walked up to his table and placed some betel leaves with a small packet of betel nuts on it. Jaiswal asked her what it was. She responded that the other day she had fainted, and she could not thank him properly for finding out what had happened to her son.

'I have come to thank you,' she said. The betel leaf and betel nuts were all she could say 'thank you' with.

Jaiswal was speechless. Never had he received a more precious expression of gratitude. After a moment had passed quietly by, he asked her if she needed any other help.

She said all she wanted was to say 'thank you' and nothing else. She folded her hands and left. Recovering from the silence of her leaving, Jaiswal instructed that her ticket back home be bought and given to her. Also, she should be escorted to the bus stand and safely seated on a bus.

Someone from his office ran after her.

13

The Murder That Wasn't

Murappanadu village is on the banks of the Thamarabarani river. The police station there sits amid the paddy fields. The village lies behind the police station and the fields stretch out in front of it. Big trees, mostly neem, loom over the station. It is the last police station on National Highway 7A in Tuticorin district. Beyond that lies Tirunelveli district.

Superintendent Jaiswal was on his way to inspect a parade in Tirunelveli when on the wireless came a message about a murder in the Murappanadu police station limits. They had crossed the police station only a while back. While returning to Tuticorin, the wireless said the local area deputy superintendent of police was on his way to the police station. A murder investigation, categorized as a grave crime, had to be supervised by the deputy superintendent of police.

Since the Murappanadu police station was on the way, Jaiswal had his car stopped there, and the moment the sentry saw the car, he stood at attention. Four or five people were sitting on the verandah as Jaiswal strode into the police station. Among them was a girl who was crying inconsolably. The inspector was there, and he stood up as soon as he saw the SP.

'What information do you have regarding the murder?' the superintendent asked without preliminaries. The inspector pointed to a woman in her forties, sitting quietly on the floor. 'She quarrelled with her husband and has murdered him,' he said.

She was wearing a saree that was old and worn out. There was, Jaiswal noticed, a tear in her blouse as well. The body was at the spot where the man had been killed in their house. The inquest was over, and they were waiting for a hired van to send the body for post-mortem to the government hospital. The murder weapon had been seized – a small short-handled axe that women used to chop firewood. The inspector requested the superintendent to sit down while he sent for a cup of tea. They were registering the FIR. Usually, police bring all the information they can into the report. It is the only document signed by the complainant. They usually got witnesses to narrate the crime coherently and obtained their signatures. Getting independent witnesses was difficult because people were hesitant to go to the court when the case came up for hearing a year or two later. The man who had been killed was short-tempered and a drunkard. Both the husband and wife worked as labourers in the fields. Outside their one-room hut they had a very small patch of land, about a fourth of an acre, in which she grew some vegetables. They had a daughter who had come of age. She was twelve or thirteen years old.

The couple fought often. If the woman didn't give him the money he asked for, he abused her and beat her in front of their daughter. If she gave him the money, he would drink and come home, and then want to have sex with his wife, and it did not bother him that the daughter was in the room. This was the pattern. If she didn't comply, he would beat her, punch her, kick her. He was violent when he was drunk, and violent when he wasn't. He would beat his daughter when she tried to defend her mother.

About six months ago, when his wife refused to let him have sex with her saying the daughter was in the room, and she was a big girl now and it was not proper, he said, 'Okay. If you refuse, she is there,' and he lurched towards the daughter. It was not clear what his intention was. He cursed the girl, picked up his sickle and swung the weapon. The girl screamed and moved away, but not before the sickle cut her on the left leg, below her knee, leaving a bleeding gash that ran deep into her calf. Screaming, the mother and daughter ran, and were able to get the wound attended to locally. It had taken six months to heal. Though the wound had healed, the girl now walked with a limp.

The night before he was killed, the man had come back drunk and lustily tried to grab his wife. She had resisted, and he had landed a couple of blows on her. She pushed him away, and he fell on the floor. He sat up and told her that if she did not do as he wanted, he would go for his daughter, and this time he would finish the job, not leave it partly done like the last time. The daughter screamed and ran to the mother and stood behind her. The man managed to get up and picked the sickle and staggered towards the daughter, shouting at her. His wife did not think twice. She picked up the short-handled axe and brought it down on her husband. Twice. The first blow landed near the right eye, and the blade took off the man's ear, and even as he began screaming, she brought the axe down again, this time harder. The axe entered the neck at an angle and went in deeper as the man flailed his arms and managed to grab her blouse before falling heavily. The frayed blue blouse, many years old, the fabric weakened by many hard washes, gave way, and a part of it came away in his hand as he bled in spurts. The girl screamed, and both ran out of the house.

When the screams drew the people from the nearby houses, they found the floor was covered in blood, the man's neck halfway cut open, the collarbone glistening white, his legs twisted below him, the sickle in his open palm, the blade of the axe buried deep in his neck. His eyes were wide open, staring at the starless night through the open door.

The wife told the neighbours she had killed her husband. It was around half past eight at night when they reached the Murappanadu police station. Only a police constable was there. He went on the wireless and informed the sub-inspector, who came later in the night. The inspector was informed, and the FIR was written, that there was a family quarrel and she killed him in the course of the quarrel and she had confessed to it and to the neighbours who were recorded as witnesses. Under the law, a confession by a criminal to the police was not admissible in court. So, the police, in the FIR, normally try to bring in witnesses so the confession would hold up in court at the time of the trial.

The wife became an accused under Section 302, which was murder. The superintendent spoke briefly with the woman. She said she knew she would be hanged for killing her husband, but she didn't care.

'I don't care if my husband had attacked me with the aruval,' she told the superintendent, adding, 'I don't mind death. But my daughter? What has she done to deserve this fate?'

Tears flowed down her face. Who would look after her daughter when she went to prison? What would become of her? The woman was only worried about her daughter.

The superintendent told the inspector that perhaps they were looking at the incident the wrong way. Life was much larger than the law. It was not murder that she was guilty of. The only eyewitness was the daughter. What had she said?

The inspector said they had not taken her statement. He asked where the daughter was. She was in the verandah and when summoned, she ran in weeping and went and hugged her mother. The girl probably thought the police would take her away, too. The inspector calmed her, gave her some tea, and spoke to her gently and she was able to narrate the incident. She showed the scar on her leg. The scar was an angry red line on her calf. She said she was afraid her father would have killed her, and she had run to her mother for protection. The superintendent asked the inspector to record the girl's statement.

After he had recorded it, he asked, 'Where is the murder now? It is pure and simple self-defence. Under law, if someone was attempting to kill another person while you are a witness, you can intervene and cause the death of the assailant to protect the other person from being murdered and that would amount to self-defence, too.'

Just a few months ago, her husband had caused an injury to his daughter with the sole intent of causing her grievous harm. He had been constantly threatening to kill their daughter, and from the pattern of his violence and cruelty to his wife and daughter, there was no doubt in his wife's mind that her husband was going to kill the daughter and afterwards, possibly her too. By her action, she had defended the life of her daughter. She did everything necessary to protect her daughter. She warned him and he hadn't listened. He had picked up the sickle with the intent to kill their daughter, and there was no reason for the wife to believe he wouldn't because he had already attempted it once. It was more than a threat. It was imminent and immediate danger to the life of her daughter. Her daughter was still limping because of the previous attack. The woman's action was preventive, not punitive, not premeditated. Her bona fide as her daughter's defender was not in question. There was no one else there to protect her daughter, to come to her aid. She was not a criminal. A broader view was called for, covered under self-defence.

The superintendent instructed that she should not be arrested. The DSP, Chockalingam, arrived when the daughter was narrating the story.

'No, sir,' he said, 'The court should decide, not us. Who are we to decide. Why should not the court decide?'

The superintendent asked him, 'Suppose a crowd is attacking and the police open fire, won't you conduct an enquiry? Do you prosecute them? Once you accept self-defence, where is the prosecution? The court will only decide when the prosecution is launched. We will register it under Section 302. We will record what happened here, as it happened, and say as per the sequence of events no murder was discovered, only preventive action by a mother to save the life of her daughter. We will put that in the FIR and send it to the court. There is nothing much to do here. The FIR has to go to the court. The case will go for closure to the court.'

Chockalingam kept quiet. The inspector wanted to talk to the DIG. Then the DIG, Jaffer Ali, called Jaiswal and said, 'Shouldn't we leave it to the court?'

'Why, sir? Tell me, why, sir? Why should an investigating officer write a charge sheet if he doesn't want to write a charge sheet? Only thing is he has to give reasons. I have given the proceedings, because accidentally I was there.'

The DIG said, 'Okay, but consult the public prosecutor.'

The matter was referred to the public prosecutor, and Superintendent Jaiswal left the police station repeating the instruction that there should be no arrest in this case. The inspector told the woman she could go home. As he walked back to the car, the woman sat there hugging her daughter, weeping with relief.

Within a week, the case was closed. No crime had been committed.

14

Liquor Sellers of Narikinaru

There are places that never make it to any map. It is no surprise, then, that in these places, crimes, even grave ones, go unreported.

After the Government of Tamil Nadu took over the sale of liquor, whether country-made or Indian-Made Foreign Liquor (IMFL), a new wing called the Prohibition Enforcement Wing was created. It was a little strange, but a state without prohibition had a prohibition enforcement wing in each and every district. Its primary task was to ensure that there was no illegal or private brewing of liquor because that would affect sales in the government's liquor outlets, and therefore, reduce revenue.

The government would often determine whether the police were doing their job properly, not on the basis of illegal brewing, but by monitoring the sale of liquor in government outlets. Had sales gone down, or gone up?

If sales dipped in any particular district or area, it was presumed that it was because of illegal brewing that was going on there and people were buying the illicitly brewed liquor, which was cheaper. There was pressure on police to conduct raids in areas where sales had fallen.

The police chased after the village-level brewing of liquor. In the villages, the method was very simple. Powdered jaggery, mixed with navacharam, a kind of salt, and water, ordinary tube-well water, was left to ferment in a drum for two or three days. They used natural fermentation agents, not yeast. The bark of the marudam tree worked well as yeast. The tree grew locally and the mixture would ferment for two or three days and after that in mud pots or aluminium pots, it was boiled on a gentle flame.

When it started steaming, they covered it with another, larger pot, into which cold water was poured, and through a funnel, the alcohol, which evaporated at seventy or eighty degrees, cooled by the cold water falling on the larger pot, condensed out in drops into a third pot. The alcohol collected was between twenty per cent or thirty per cent proof. Minimum twenty per cent. This was sold.

Many times, the customers would ask, 'Is it the first wash or the second wash?' The second wash would be the remnants of the first wash processed again. The first wash was stronger than the second.

At Narikinaru, Jaiswal came to know that there was large-scale illicit brewing going on.

When alcohol is brewed, some of it escapes into the

air and you can smell it for miles around; you can tell that alcohol is being brewed in the vicinity. When the police came to know, they went to raid the village. Thirty or forty policemen went to Narikinaru in a bus and in jeeps. The dwellings were scattered, less than a hundred of them. The minute the villagers came to know police were doing a raid, the whole village became almost instantly deserted. All went out into the fields and stood in groups and watched the police from afar.

In the bigger houses, the police found drums of wash. Every hut they entered had two or three pots of wash lying in some corner or the other. Some fires that had not been put out greeted the police and in many of the houses, food lay uneaten as the villagers had abandoned the plates and ran away.

From Narikinaru, all the men had left to find work or a life elsewhere. Only the elderly among the men remained, and the very young. There weren't enough men even to work in the fields. Women worked in the fields.

It was literally home-brew. After the meal was prepared, the woman of the house would sit down at the same hearth, brew and then distil alcohol. If she got two bottles of alcohol, she was done for the day. Two was the maximum. Each woman added her own flavouring agent, like ripe banana or orange.

These women tied the alcohol bottles with strings to their waist and kept them hidden under their lower garment, the pavadai (the underskirt of the saree). They would take the bus, go out into the market, not in their own village, but to one of the weekly markets, a Wednesday market or a Thursday market, in the nearby villages. They would sell it there in small cups or glasses.

Jaiswal's raiding party informed him that this method of selling alcohol had a sensual touch, too. The women had to lift their pavadai and then pour the alcohol into cups, and the men who bought alcohol this way had their favourites, either the flash of thigh or the taste of the hooch, or the combination. There was no standardization but the regular customers knew which woman would sell what kind of alcohol. They often waited and bought alcohol from the woman they preferred.

It was very difficult for the police to check the illicit alcohol traffic if it was done this way. Frisking women was a dicey business, unless there were enough women constables to do it, and so the villagers of Narikinaru usually plied their business unhindered and undetected.

The poverty that Jaiswal could see all around him was stark and dismal. This cottage industry helped the villagers to survive while the fields lay almost fallow due to the lack of workforce and other earnings were also meagre.

The police broke the pots they found with the washes, especially from the bigger houses. Looking at the miserable trail of destruction that they were leaving behind, Jaiswal felt wretched after a while. What could be a bigger crime against Narikinaru except for the crushing poverty that he saw all around? Jaiswal ordered the police back into the vehicles, their job only partially done, and the men in uniform headed back to civilization, leaving Narikinaru to itself.

15

Ganiammal

Have I told you about Ganiammal? Ganiammal was known at the Town South police station as a characterless woman. You couldn't say she was attractive, but she had a strong personality. Full of confidence, cheeky, vivacious and bursting with life.

That was before she fell into bad times. She sold flowers at the Sivan Koil, the biggest temple in the area, on the West Great Cotton Road in Tuticorin. She had married a small-time rowdy and had a small girl and was carrying another child that would soon be born.

So, she couldn't go out for the kind of work that had earned her the sobriquet 'characterless'. She was deft at stringing jasmine flowers with thread. Her husband came and went as he pleased in the hut she stayed. One evening while she slept, he rummaged through the mud pot in which she stored rice and found five hundred rupees that she had kept hidden. It was all the money she had to buy flowers for the next day, including three hundred and fifty rupees she owed on credit for flowers, and all her savings. He took the money and went away. In the morning when Ganiammal found the money missing, she howled. Then she went to the police station but was chased away. Eventually she found her way to Superintendent Jaiswal's camp office.

There were already some visitors who were waiting to air their complaints.

The superintendent of police was inside his house. The Special Branch inspector had come to meet him and he heard her arguing outside the gate. The Special Branch inspector went out and then the superintendent of police could hear him shouting at the top of his voice at someone and chasing her away using expletives.

Normally, no one raised their voice in front of the SP's residence, especially the policemen, and Jaiswal came out, still in his kurta pyjama, and Mini, his daughter, came running out to see what the excitement was all about. In one hand, she held her favourite toy, and with the other hand, she held on to her father.

Seeing the superintendent and his daughter, the inspector stopped shouting. He explained, 'She is a very bad woman, very foul-mouthed, sir. She is complaining she cannot go for her regular business because of her pregnancy. She is asking policemen for money, saying she will repay them when her pregnancy is over and her child born.'

'Wait a minute,' Jaiswal told the Special Branch inspector, 'What can be a bigger insult to the SP, if someone says she will take up prostitution if no one can help her?'

Jaiswal beckoned the woman forward. As she walked to him, her child held on to her. She told him her name and the story of how her savings had gone missing. All the while her child kept looking at Mini's toy and Mini must have noticed it and she wanted to introduce her toy to the child. But her father asked her to go inside and eat her breakfast, and later perhaps, she could introduce her toy. Now, he had work to do. Mini smiled brightly and waved goodbye, and went back inside.

Jaiswal offered to have a case registered against her husband.

Ganiammal protested.

'But I don't want a case. What will I do with a case? I want my money back. If you want to help me, send your policemen and catch him. I know where that loafer will be. You will find my money with him and you can give it back to me. That's all I want.'

More to get rid of her than anything, Jaiswal asked that a couple of policemen go in the jeep along with Ganiammal and bring her husband to the camp office, if he was where she thought he would be. She got into the jeep with her child and they went away.

Once they were gone, the Special Branch inspector told him Ganiammal's story. Whenever a particular minister came to visit, she was called for the night to keep him entertained. Once she had raun away with the gold chain that the minister had worn around his neck. She had asked him to remove it during their time together, saying it was getting in the way, and he was drunk enough that night to do it. When he fell asleep, Ganiammal took the chain and left. In the morning, the minister was furious when he saw the necklace gone along with Ganiammal. He shouted at everybody around him. A Special Branch inspector was sent to retrieve the chain.

Ganiammal refused to return the chain unless she was paid for all the things she had done for the minister during his previous three visits when she had been sent to spend the nights with him. The minister was particular that she alone come to his room when he visited. No other woman. He always asked for her. Ganiammal proceeded to recount the minister's sexual kinks graphically, rounding off each episode with how much do you think I need to be paid for doing that? The acts she detailed were so lurid and kinky that even the tough Special Branch inspector had blushed as he tried to cajole her into accepting secret funds money to assuage her. Even though the minister kept asking for her during his subsequent visits, Ganiammal refused.

She sent the police emissaries away saying even animals had better manners.

Ganiammal returned about an hour later with her husband. It must have been half past eight in the morning. He was already drunk. He had exactly thirty-two rupees in his pocket. He had repaid all the debts he had accumulated with the money he had stolen and with the remaining, he bought himself alcohol and drank it. When the police found him, he had been lying on the side of the road, slurring.

Jaiswal ordered that he be taken to the police station and charged under Section 75 of the Tamil Nadu Police City Act. This pertained to breach of peace in a public place. It was a provision that covered common drunks. They took him to the police station, tied a chain around his leg, and left him there to sober up.

Ganiammal was crestfallen. She started howling loudly, 'What am I to do now? I need the money. I earned the money in a clean way, selling flowers, not in any other way. I cannot earn money the way I normally do. I have a child to feed. What do I do now?'

'Amma, ippo summa iru. Ukkaru angey' (Let us see what can be done. For the moment keep quiet and sit there), Jaiswal told her.

Grumbling, she sat down where Jaiswal had pointed. He went home and showered, changed into his uniform, ate his breakfast and went to the camp office. He had no sooner sat down than the constable came in with a card which he kept on the table.

Jaiswal saw it was from the Canara Bank manager and asked that he be shown in. The manager had told the superintendent of police that the bank had applied for a gun licence for the security guard of the bank and the matter had been pending for a long time. Could he do something about it?

'You are a real avatar of Lord Shiva!' responded Jaiswal. 'As far as the gun licence is concerned, I will personally go to the collector and see that it is issued. But you have to solve a grave problem for me.'

'What is it, sir?'

'I have a woman waiting outside who is threatening that she will take the wrong road if she doesn't get five hundred rupees. Why don't you give her a small loan?'

'I don't understand, sir.'

Jaiswal explained the situation to him and told him that Ganiammal sold flowers at the Sivan Koil.

Banks usually gave loans at differential interest rates to very poor people – people who often found the bureaucracy daunting and forbidding – under the DIR scheme. Jaiswal told the bank manager that he could interview the candidate right there. The bank manager agreed to meet her and Ganiammal was called in. She came in holding her little girl by the shoulder.

After seeing her, he looked at Jaiswal and asked, 'Will she repay?'

Jaiswal told Ganiammal, 'Intha aiyyah, Canara Bank aiyyah. Kadan kuduparu ainooru rubai. Methuva methuva ninko thiruppi kodakkanum. Okayva?' (He is an officer from the bank and he will loan you five hundred rupees and you should repay it little by little.)

'Kandippa aiyyah, naan thiruppi tharuven.' (Definitely, sir. I will return the money.)

The manager asked her to come to the bank, telling her that if she returned the money, he would loan a bigger amount. There ended one phase of Jaiswal's interaction with Ganiammal.

Six months later, one evening while Jaiswal was sitting

with Neelam on the chairs they had placed under the portico. Ganiammal came again. She looked different, in a lapis lazuli blue saree and flowers in her hair and a big pottu, bindi, on her forehead. She carried a baby boy in her arms as the older child stood behind her.

Jaiswal asked her how she was and if her husband was giving her any trouble. She said no, her husband was now a different person, and he was living with her. She had come with some information. She said it was urgent.

In the slums in which she lived, in the lane behind her home, illicit liquor was being stored. That evening, a van had come and illicit liquor was loaded into it, one jerry can after another. She didn't know where it had come from, and neither did she know where it was going to be taken. But the air in the area was thick with the smell of hooch. She urged that the police be sent there immediately. Tuticorin was awash with illicit liquor. Fishermen could easily take it in boats and unload it anywhere along the coast, all the way down to Kanyakumari or up the coast. There were no barriers or checkposts in the sea.

Jaiswal asked her why she was passing this information. If the people in the trade came to know, what would happen to her and her children? She responded that since he had helped her with the loan, she felt obliged to help in some way. But, now, she agreed that she might get into trouble for the tip she had passed on.

'Ammam, aiyyah. Theruvula yellarkum theriyum neenga yennakku uthavi pannirkirengo.' (Yes, sir. Everyone in the streets knows that you have helped me out.)

'So, how will this help you?'

She had a plan. She said, 'Can you tell the inspector whom you send to seize the illicit liquor to beat me with a stick once or twice in front of everybody. That should allay any suspicions.'

Jaiswal got a constable to note down the exact location where the consignment was being loaded and sent Ganiammal away. He summoned Inspector Ponnuswamy, who was a tough police personnel, a terror from the Tuticorin North Police Station limits. Jaiswal gave him the location and asked him to catch the consignment. He ended the conversation by saying that he was getting some complaints that Ganiammal was quarrelling with people and creating a nuisance, and asked him to warn her to behave better.

Ponnuswamy managed to seize the lorry and picked up two or three people. While he was doing this, before moving the lorry to the police station, Ganiammal had come out of her hut and began shouting at Inspector Ponnuswamy, ridiculing him, saying that there would be no case, there was nothing to worry, all that would happen was the lorry would be taken to the police station, some money would change hands and everything would be fine. 'Eh! Summa iru ni' (Keep quiet, woman), Inspector Ponnuswamy warned Ganiammal. 'Podanga porki, ni yennathan pudungaporai!' (You are no better than a rowdy. What are you capable of, nothing!) Then, she spat in his direction. A blob of her spittle landed on Inspector Ponnuswamy's shoe. With his thick lathi, he dealt her a blow. She retaliated further with a stream of expletives. Inspector Ponnuswamy lost his temper. He started to hit her with the lathi repeatedly, five, six, maybe ten times. Screaming, she ran away. Ponnuswamy took the lorry with forty jerry cans of illicit liquor and went away. He then called the SP to say the raid had been successful. He did not tell Jaiswal anything about the altercation. It must have been after eleven, and Jaiswal had retired to the residence when the guard rang the bell and said the woman who had come earlier in the evening was back. He asked him what she wanted?

'Aiyyah, yaro adichutango avala, nalla adi pattirukku aval mela!' (Sir, someone has beaten her badly. She is covered with bruises.) Jaiswal assumed that the liquor mafia had caught her and beaten her up. He came out and Ganiammal was standing in front of him with her two children.

'Yenna achchu?' he asked Ganiammal. 'What happened?'

She started smiling and said 'Naan ungalai oru rendu adi thaane kodakka sonnein? Yevallo adi naan vankinein? Evalo adi ninga koduthel, athu nyama ma saar?' (I asked that I be beaten only once or twice, but how many blows I have received! Is it fair?)

Jaiswal called for driver Kanakaraj, told him to take her to the nearest hospital and have her injuries attended to. She was taken there and her wounds were cleaned and medicated and in one or two places, bandaged, and she was back in an hour. He went into the camp office and called her there. When she came in, Jaiswal opened the drawer where he kept secret service funds and pulled out some money, maybe six hundred or seven hundred rupees, from the secret fund, and attempted to give it to her. She stood with folded hands, refusing to take the money.

'Aiyyah, naan kaasukage pannale. Aiyyah, mannikanam. Ungalakku nalla paer vaaranamnuthan naan pannen. Yennakku intha kaasu vendam. Neenga pannina uthaviye pothum.' (I didn't give you information for money, sir. I will not take it, please forgive me. I did it, so that you could get a good name. I don't want this money. The help you had given me is enough.) 'Naan athuliye pozhaichupein.' (I will get by with that alone.)

She turned and walked out of the camp office with her children.

Jaiswal asked the bank if they could, under the innovative banking scheme, finance an autorickshaw for Ganiammal's husband. Three or four months later they did finance an autorickshaw in her name, not her husband's. She had already made a good reputation by repaying her earlier loans little by little, steadily. She missed her instalments only when she fell ill and could not sell flowers. But by and large she had a good record. Her husband would drive the rickshaw but the rickshaw would belong to her. He was only the driver.

That was the last time Jaiswal heard anything from her. He left Tuticorin and went to the Intelligence Bureau in Delhi and found himself back in Tamil Nadu after fourteen years. He lived in the IG quarters in Wallajah Road, near the cricket stadium. Mini had been very ill. Cancer was claiming her. She didn't have much time left, maybe just a few months. Those were very difficult days, harrowing.

One morning the bell rang, and Jaiswal was informed that a woman had come and wanted to meet him. It was Ganiammal. Her son, now grown up, was with her. She was neatly dressed and wore jasmine flowers in her hair, the smell of which wafted around the room. Jaiswal was pleasantly surprised. How did she know that he was in Chennai? She informed him that she saw in the local papers in Tuticorin a picture of Jaiswal, in uniform, taking a parade somewhere. She had made enquiries and immediately taken the train and come to Chennai. From the guards downstairs, she had come to know about Mini's illness.

Ganiammal requested Jaiswal to keep her in his house as house help and she would also cook. I am clean now, sir, she kept assuring him. 'I am a clean woman, I am a clean woman'. All Jaiswal could do was to stand in front of her, with folded hands, and thank her.

16

Life After Death

The *Chippi* ('shell' in Tamil) was a small vessel owned by the Central Marine and Fisheries Research Institute (CMFRI). Off the Tuticorin coast, women, and later men, dived for oyster shells from the bed of the Gulf of Mannar. *Chippi* collected marine specimens for research, pottering around slowly in the aquamarine sea around Tuticorin, with its outboard motor making a racket.

The CMFRI was doing research on edible oysters and pearl oysters. They had scuba diving equipment and their divers collected samples. These waters were ideal for snorkelling and scuba diving. Jaiswal learnt both because of the CMFRI.

Once *Chippi* found a suitable spot, its anchor was lowered and a big stone was tied to a rope and thrown into the water. Wearing the scuba diving equipment, divers held on to the rope and went down, breathing through an aqualung.

That is how Jaiswal learnt to dive, at depths of ten or

fifteen feet under the sea. It was an old lady's sport, they said. You didn't need to know swimming. All you needed to do was to learn to breathe through the mouth, and for that, there was a mouthpiece. You went down into the sea, breathing through the mouth. The same went for the snorkels. You breathed through your mouth, the air came in through the tube that went by your ear and stayed above the water. Once you wore the mask, life in the water came alive, while you floated, face-down, in the water, the air coming in through the tube which was above the water.

The Institute started the Pearl City Adventure Club. For students, it was ten rupees per year and for adults, it was hundred rupees and there was a patron's fee. It was cheap because the trips were funded; the kerosene for the trips was funded by SPIC and breakfast by Madura Coats. There was a building where it was located and Jaiswal was the president of the club for a while. The club taught children and adults snorkelling and scuba diving. Madura Coats helped the club fund the equipment, and SPIC helped it to buy a couple of fibreglass boats.

Originally, these boats had been seized by customs when they had come in from Sri Lanka. The customs department often seized boats that were used by smugglers and later they sold the boats in auction. In the auction, the club participated; it got the boats for the price it wanted.

Patrons went out diving on Saturdays and Sundays. Off Tuticorin, in the Gulf of Mannar, were a series of coral islands, going all the way north up to Rameswaram, in the curve of the peninsula. There were some 21 or 22 of those reefs, nearly 200 kilometres by the road along the coast. Near Tuticorin, the most well known was the island of Muyaldeep, which had an aerostrip, then Vaanadeep, Kaswar, Challideep, Upputhanni Deep, Nallathanni Deep, and these stretched like pearls flung in an arc, all the way up to Kursadai island in Rameswaram. Kurusadai was a very big coral reef island. That was where the headquarters of the CMFRI was located in the Gulf of Mannar.

It was off Vaanadeep that they went for snorkelling. If the sea was rough on one side of the island, the other side was calm as a sheet of glass. It was so beautiful that sometimes one was mesmerized by the coral paradise.

In 1987–88, an assistant superintendent of police under training arrived in Tuticorin. His name was Phillip. The only swimming Phillip knew was what he had learnt in the police academy, which was basic, and neither here nor there. He wanted to go snorkelling and one weekend, twenty of them reached Vaanadeep on two fibreglass motorboats.

Antony Pichai, a retired diver from CMFRI, was the coach. If you went diving with him and if you did everything in the right way, he would smile at you when you came up afterwards. If you did something wrong, when you came up, he would still smile, but the smile would be a wide one. Both right and wrong were conveyed by the width of his smile. Antony Pichai did not once, even once, say you had done something incorrectly.

It was the first time for Phillip and Jaiswal told Antony

to be with the ASP. Antony took Phillip for a long round out in the lagoon, told him how to wear the mask, wash it in the seawater before he strapped it on, and practise breathing many times. They had done one round and then Pichai had brought him back to the shore. Pichai instructed him not to venture out alone without someone accompanying him.

Once on the shore, Antony Pichai began preparing for a second round when somebody else, a schoolboy, drew Antony's attention, and he went to help him. The boy had seen a flower blooming at a depth of two feet. Whenever he reached out to touch it, the flower was not there. Was it an illusion? It was a sea anemone, Antony explained. The anemone withdrew its tentacles whenever it sensed the boy's hand approaching.

Phillip, meanwhile, thinking that he now had everything under control and had learnt what he needed to, set out for another round of snorkelling, alone. The sea didn't look deep, and it was calm, and it had been so easy. He went without telling anyone.

Vaanadeep was not a big island and all twenty divers were scattered around in an area of not more than fifty yards. Jaiswal could not see Phillip anywhere. 'Where is Phillip? Where is Phillip?' he asked loudly. Antony Pichai pointed in the direction he had left him and said, 'There!'

But Jaiswal couldn't see Phillip.

Suddenly another boy, Pradeep, began shouting, 'Sir, sir!' pointing at something. It was the red swimwear Phillip had been wearing. Only his buttocks were above the water, the head and legs in a V, under the water, a typical sign of drowning.

Jaiswal shouted, 'Jump jump, get him!' There was a head constable who was in line with the floating body. He jumped in and was the first to reach Phillip, and he dragged him out, while Jaiswal shouted, 'Pull his head up, pull his head up!' The head constable reached the shore with Phillip, dragged him out, and stretched him on the beach. He kept repeating, 'Intha Kathai mutinchurthu.' (His story has ended.)

When Jaiswal saw Phillip, there was froth on his face and blood dribbling out of his nose and mouth. His body was limp, his stomach distended. He was without his snorkelling mask. Jaiswal's legs started to tremble. He didn't know what to do.

A week ago, Jaiswal's daughter had been unable to sleep. While she lay awake, he had sat by her side, reading some book on snorkelling, and then he had put it away and had for some reason begun reading a book about drowning.

It said the sea is far more merciful to those who are drowning than rivers or fresh water bodies. When a person drowns in fresh water, a river or a pond or a well or a lake, the lungs get flooded with water. Being less dense than blood, the water in the lungs, through osmotic pressure, oozes into the bloodstream, leading to hypo-dilution of the blood. It triggers a chemical reaction that causes the heart to stop instantly and leads to instant death.

But seawater is denser than blood. When seawater floods the lungs, hyperconcentration occurs. The water or plasma from the blood starts oozing into the lungs, and the blood becomes thicker and thicker and the heart has to pump harder and harder and it takes a few minutes for the heart to stop. Compared to fresh water, seawater takes a few more minutes to kill a person.

All this flashed through Jaiswal's mind when he jumped to the ground and started pressing Phillip's chest, trying to revive him. It didn't work. Then Jaiswal asked two of the policemen who were with them to lift Phillip by his legs and hold him upside down. Two people caught each of Phillip's legs and lifted him and while someone else held his knees, Jaiswal knelt down and began squeezing Phillip's lungs with all his might. Seawater began spurting out of Phillip's mouth and upturned nose along with specks of blood and froth. When water no longer came out of him, they lay him down on the ground again and Jaiswal virtually began jumping on his chest, pressing it very hard. Every time he pressed Phillip's lungs, air came out of his mouth emitting a hoarse sound like a crow with a bad lung condition, and when the pressure eased, the air would go back in but then it would stop. There was no pulse.

Again and again, Jaiswal repeated this. He was about to give up, when he pushed on his chest for the last time, there was a sound, a loud sound, that went phaakkkk, like something had been freed inside Phillip. All of a sudden, when Jaiswal eased the pressure, he found Phillip taking in a breath on his own. He continued to press on Phillip's chest and he started sustaining it, and after thirty or forty seconds,

Phillip started taking breaths on his own, five or six of them. They turned him to his side, and more fluid started coming out of his mouth, and Phillip started moaning. At first, it was like a cry of agony. He started wailing and moaning as if he was in great distress. His breathing was irregular.

By that time, Jaiswal was sweating profusely. 'Uzhir irukku!' (He's alive!), he said, but what damage had occurred he did not know and could not say. Somebody suggested they should immediately put Phillip in a boat and take him to a hospital, but Jaiswal suggested otherwise. He was of the opinion that if there was a relapse there would be no way to revive him.

He said they should wait a while to see if Phillip stabilized. Somebody lit a cigarette for Jaiswal but he was too nervous to smoke. As they waited, Phillip's breathing became regular. Jaiswal got on the wireless and asked that an ambulance be brought to the shore and kept waiting. Meanwhile they started readying the boat to put Phillip on it.

Phillip's eyes fluttered open about a quarter of an hour later. He looked around him and immediately began to vomit. Then he tried to sit up and kept looking at his fingers. Looking at Jaiswal, he asked, 'Where is the ring? Where is the ring? Where is the SP?'

He tried to sit up again. They laid a small mattress out on the boat for Phillip and headed back to Tuticorin.

Phillip was admitted not into a government hospital but to Rajam's Clinic, run by Jaiswal's friend, Dr Ravindran. By that time, his snorkelling mask had been recovered. Phillip had managed to take off the mask by snapping it with great force during his death throes.

Jaiswal asked Phillip what had happened. Phillip said, weakly, he had felt very confident. He decided to go for a small swim on his own. His head was facing the seabed, and he did not know in which direction he was heading. The water looked very shallow. Maybe he kicked his fin harder, and he went in deeper. The seabed looked near, due to the higher refractive index of salt water. He saw the bottom of the sea was very near and he thought he would stand up for a while. He tried to let his legs go down so he could stand up. But he couldn't feel the sand beneath his feet. He tried to come back to the snorkelling position again, but he couldn't. The snorkelling tube went underwater and got filled with water. When Phillip tried to breathe, salt water filled his mouth. He found he couldn't breathe. He had a vision of his parents as he realized that he was drowning.

Phillip told Jaiswal, 'I thought I called out to you to save me. "Save me! Save me!" I kept shouting. Then I don't know what happened. I was feeling like many people were trying to drown me. They were pushing me into the water, pushing me down. Drown! Drown! Drown! I was struggling, trying not to drown, but there were ten or fifteen people holding me, pressing me under the water, drowning me.'

Twenty days later, Phillip was to be married in Bangalore.

That was the first of several miraculous near-death experiences that Jaiswal saw during his tenure in Tuticorin.

As superintendent of police, one of Jaiswal's duties was to go for night rounds. For this, Jaiswal would choose any subdivision, maybe drive for an hour to Kovilpatti and stay there till midnight or one o'clock and then come back.

There was only one condition for the SP to keep in mind. The element of surprise was always there. It was to check if the shifts were going on regularly, if the patta books were signed. In the police station, there would be a small book hanging by a string. The policemen in the night shift had to come and sign the book and mention the time when it was signed. Senior officers and inspectors regularly checked this book. The SP also went around the roads, and if he spotted any policemen, he called them to find out what work they were doing, which police station they were from. The SP would also read their diary where the policemen made entries of what they had observed in the night or whether they had noticed anybody loitering. It was not that people couldn't walk around, but there had to be a good reason for a person to be out late at night, and if the person was carrying a bag it was important to see what he was carrying in it.

After one such night round, Jaiswal was returning home. It was well past midnight. On Ettayapuram road, there was a T-junction, and if you turned right, it would take you to State Bank Colony where Jaiswal's camp office was, and there was a petrol pump open through the night. Opposite to it were some repair shops and hotels which were open till late in the night. There was a small crowd on the road and Jaiswal asked the driver to stop and find out what was going on.

The driver stopped the car and ran there and came back immediately, saying there had been an accident and someone had been killed. Jaiswal got out of the car and went to the spot, and saw a man lying in a pool of blood under the street light. His motorcycle was on top of him. They said the man had come at high speed and hit a pipe that had been projecting on the road. He had not seen it. He flew into the air as did the motorcycle. He fell and the motorcycle fell on top of him. He was dead, they said.

Jaiswal immediately said he would call the control room. He went back to the car to call on the wireless, and before he could press the mike, it occurred to him, 'How do we know the man is dead?'

He rushed back to the man lying on the ground and tried to feel his pulse. One of his hands was under the motorcycle and the other pinned behind his back. Jaiswal prised his hand out from behind him. He could feel a strong pulse. The man was not dead. There was a truck standing there. With the help of the bystanders, they loaded him into the truck and asked the truck to be taken to the hospital behind the Town South Police Station.

Jaiswal rushed to the wireless and called the Town South Police Station and told them that he was sending a critically injured person by truck to the hospital behind the police station and instructed that the night duty policemen should immediately go to the hospital and tell the hospital outpost to get the emergency doctor and the emergency room ready. He instructed that a constable should stay behind in the hospital to see if blood was required, for the man had lost a lot of blood. There were records in police stations of a list of donors with their blood groups for precisely such situations. By the time the truck reached the hospital, the doctors were ready to receive the injured man.

Three days later, Jaiswal got a message that the man had been removed from the ICU and was out of danger. A month later, the man came to the camp office with a box of sweets.

An even more bizarre case occurred on the national highway around the same period. Jaiswal had a problem with his eye. There was a stye, which was irritating his left eye. He suffered it for a few days thinking it would become all right on its own. Then a friend told him he knew someone at the Arvind Eye Hospital in Madurai who had fixed a similar problem for him, and that Jaiswal should go there and have it attended to. Jaiswal took a bus to Madurai.

There his counterpart, Shekhar, who later became DGP, was the SP. Jaiswal had told him he was coming there, and Shekhar had sent a vehicle to the bus stand to receive Jaiswal to take him to the hospital. He left in the afternoon and was there by four thirty or so. The doctor removed the stye within ten minutes, using local anaesthesia. He bandaged Jaiswal's eye and said the bandage could be removed after an hour or so.

The Madurai SP let Jaiswal take his vehicle back home to Tuticorin.

Somewhere down the highway the traffic came to a halt. There was a long line of vehicles which had halted on the left side of the road. Dusk was falling. They waited for a few minutes and then Jaiswal told the driver, 'Look, this is a police vehicle, there is no divider. Get on the right lane and let us see how far we can go.'

They drove on and stopped where the problem began at a point where a kutcha road met the highway. There were two policemen standing there, and Jaiswal got out of the vehicle and asked the policemen what the problem was. He was told that it was a hit-and-run case. Somebody walking on the road was hit by a passing vehicle and the man fell dead. They pointed to where the victim lay. He was there in the middle of the road. Around him was a white mark with a chalk. That meant the sub-inspector had come for the inquest and had marked the position of the body, determined what was found on the body, so it would help in the investigation.

All that remained was for the body now to be sent for post-mortem, and the inspector had gone to fetch a vehicle to ferry the body to the hospital. Jaiswal was about to walk back to his car, but on second thoughts, went to investigate the body of the accident victim more closely. He walked up to the spot and stood looking down at the body in the gathering dusk. To his surprise, he thought he saw the head jerking faintly.

Jaiswal thought his one eye was playing tricks. He kept peering at the body on the road with one eye and again

Jaiswal felt the head jerked. Jaiswal knelt down on the road and put his hands on the man's temples; he could feel a pulse. He jumped up and shouted, 'This man is alive! He is alive!'

He wanted to turn his vehicle, but there was no place to turn. Behind stood a car that had a sign saying Lakshmi Mills. Jaiswal went and introduced himself to the occupant. 'Look, sir, I am the superintendent of police, Tuticorin.' He requested them to let their vehicle take the injured man to the hospital. The occupant turned out to be the general manager of Lakshmi Mills, and he hesitated a bit, but Jaiswal guaranteed that there would be no trouble even should the man die on the way. His vehicle was headed in the right direction and there was no time to waste. The Lakshmi Mills manager agreed to vacate the car for this purpose.

Jaiswal asked the constables to load the injured man in the back seat. But they said their sub-inspector would be back. Jaiswal said there was no time and to do it now. The constable said there was a small PHC. Jaiswal dismissed the idea and told them to take the injured man to a hospital, which was fifteen kilometres away. The driver of the Lakshmi Mills car and the constables got into the car to head to the hospital, and by this time the sub-inspector had arrived.

Jaiswal told the sub-inspector that in the same van he should follow the Lakshmi Mills car and make sure things went smoothly in the hospital. The traffic eased. Jaiswal dropped the Lakshmi Mills manager in his car and gave him his phone number and told him if there was any problem, he should get in touch. Jaiswal offered to have the car washed, but the Lakshmi Mills manager declined. Jaiswal returned home and took off the bandage. Two days later, he heard the man had survived. It had been a close call. Jaiswal never saw him again. Nor did he hear from him.

17

The Safe Hands of Fate

The local inspector from the Siruvaikundam subdivision brought an accused to Tuticorin to get her admitted to the general hospital. The injuries on her were far too serious for the local PHC to manage. She was a menial labourer, with two children; the elder one was not even three years old. Her husband had abandoned her after she became pregnant for the third time.

She had developed some pregnancy-related complications and had not been able to go out for work. For a while, her neighbours had helped her out. Not being able to feed her children, and not being able to bear the sight of their hunger, she decided to end her life as well as that of her children.

She took them to an open well. It was a deep body of water, with a small bank below and a track leading down to it. The land surrounding the well rose steeply, in some places about ten to fifteen feet high. From that height, she pushed her children into the water one after the other, fighting their resistance and tears. She wept as they drowned and then threw herself into the well, too. When she hit the water, she did not drown because she could swim a little, and instinct made her pull herself out.

In the water, the bodies of her children began to float face down as the ripples settled. Seeing her dead children, she became desperate to end her life, and she climbed up again, this time to a rocky, higher bank. She jumped again. She hit the side of the bank as she fell into the water and was injured by the shrubs that grew near the outcrop; swathes of her skin were scratched off by the rock as she fell down into the water. Again, her ability to float prevented her from drowning.

She trod the ground and dragged herself up the bank, and again she jumped. This time too she didn't drown, and according to the inspector, broke her hips and suffered a miscarriage instead. She was found unconscious and bleeding and taken to the PHC. The post-mortem was done on the bodies of the children. Their deaths had been caused by drowning.

Jaiswal went to the hospital, and the doctor said she would pull through. When she could eventually talk, she blamed herself for what had happened, that she had killed her children because she had seen no hope for herself, for them or for the unborn child she had been carrying in her womb.

The inspector told the SP that he was unable to register a case against her, except attempted suicide, Section 309. It would be pathetic if he did, and he didn't want to.

'Leave it,' said Jaiswal. 'We have better cases to pursue. There is nothing much to investigate here. And what would you get out of it? We can't register a case against poverty for murdering the children and attempting to murder her, can we?'

They left her there, heavily bandaged, in plaster casts, in the general ward of the Tuticorin General Hospital, consigning her into the hands of fate.

18

The Misfit

Jaiswal had never wanted to become a policeman. When he did become one, though, from early on he was declared a misfit. It was a label that had attached itself to him, before he even realized it.

He had come out of a Sainik School and joined the National Defence Academy at Khadakvasla as a cadet, hoping to become a fighter pilot. But his mind had been colonized by his Sainik School physics teacher. The Sainik School at Ghorakhal was a boarding school for boys, an incubator for them before they joined the defence services.

In class six, Jaiswal's father had admitted him to Government Jubilee Intermediate School in Gorakhpur, Uttar Pradesh. He had built a house on a plot of forty by sixty feet in a colony adjacent to the school. For almost two years after they moved into that house there was no electricity; that amenity reached them much later.

It was an incomplete house. The entrance, the boundary

wall, the verandah, the drawing room – his father left all of it unconstructed. When they asked him about, he would laugh it away, saying he wanted a good frontage and for that he needed to save more money. The incomplete house had four rooms. Jaiswal's grandmother slept in one of them. The other rooms were best described as storage rooms.

They didn't have the concept of bedrooms and a dining space. They slept on charpoys, and wherever the charpoy was laid out became the bedroom. In the morning, when they woke up, the charpoys were rolled up and placed on one side, flush against the wall. The bathroom and the toilet were out in the back.

Jaiswal's childhood was a very happy one. The neighbourhood had plenty of children his age to keep him company. It was with reluctance that the children would return home after play.

The Government Jubilee Intermediate School building had a row of low, yellowing, single-storeyed structures, with square windows and a roof that had been red long ago but was now a dull brown. The main building had a wide verandah with arches running along it. The trees that lined the big school grounds stood taller than the school buildings. In the classroom, there were some ninety-odd children. At the back of each classroom, there were three or four rows of benches. Most students sat on the floor, wearing navy blue shorts and white shirts, which was the uniform. And the white shirts would eventually also turn blue because ink kept staining their shirts. Every morning, the peon would come with a kettle of ink and pour it into the inkpots. He must have been sloppy. There was invariably more ink on the floor, and on the hands and shirts of students than in the pot or the pens that they wrote with.

The cane that the teacher carried spoke more than the teacher, and much more eloquently, too. One whack of the cane was enough to ensure at least five minutes of pin-drop silence. Then, the whispering would crop up slowly, followed by loud chatter, before the cane descended again.

The teacher who terrified them most was Mahatham Singh. He possessed the fastest and the most painful cane in Government Jubilee Intermediate School. When he wasn't caning them, he taught mathematics. Mahatham Singh had a unique way of announcing his presence. They knew he was in the classroom because they would hear the sharp swish of the cane followed by the thwack of it cutting into somebody's back. That would be the exact moment when the classroom hubbub died away.

One day, he asked, after he had enforced silence the usual way, 'Any of you want to serve the country in the fauj (Indian Army)?' Jaiswal didn't know at the time that the question was going to change his life. The children had no concept of the army. The nearest they had come to thinking about it was during the NCC parades, which some children participated in by donning ill-fitting clothes. All kept quiet. Mahatham Singh taunted, 'Oh. So, you are a classroom full of cowards. Not a single one is brave or bold enough to serve the country in the Indian Army?'

When he called them cowards, without thinking, Jaiswal raised his hand. On a piece of paper, Mahatham Singh jotted down his name, date of birth and his father's name. Then he asked, 'Anybody else?' Two more hands shot up and their names were recorded. He said there would be examinations and that they should prepare for them. Then he continued with the class.

When Jaiswal told his parents he had opted to join the Indian Army – 'Bharatiya fauj ko join karne ke liye apna naam diya hun' (I have given my name to join the Indian Army) – they didn't pay any attention. They probably thought it was a boyhood fad. A month or so later, he was sitting in the classroom chatting with a classmate when he felt an iron rod sting his back. It was the cane. As was the custom, complete silence ensued. Jaiswal looked up to see Mahatham Singh peering down at him.

'You are Jaiswal?' he asked.

'Ji, sir.'

'Then why don't you speak up? I have been calling out your name.'

Jaiswal kept quiet.

'Get up. Get out of the class and stand in the field.'

Jaiswal went out of the classroom, and the mathematics teacher sent two more children out as well. On the road by the ground, an army truck was standing.

Mahatham Singh followed the children and ordered them into the truck. The truck was already full of children, and it went to the campus of another school. They jumped out of the truck, and on the big football field were about fifty children. There was also a blackboard, some chairs and a table standing next to them. Two men in uniform were sitting on the chairs.

The children moved to the table in a line and when Jaiswal got to the table, he found the army men were breaking pencils into two and giving each one half a pencil and an eraser, also cut in half. They were going to take an examination. On the blackboard there were about twenty-five questions.

The boys stood in rows and copied the questions on the sheets they had been given. Then, they were sent off into the field to scatter and sit and answer the questions without talking. They could take with them the pencil and the eraser when they were done. Jaiswal went home feeling happy because even if he didn't pass the exam, he had new stationery. He told his parents about the examination and showed them the pencil and the eraser. They smiled. There was no other reaction from them.

A month later, Mahatham Singh called out Jaiswal's name in the classroom and asked him to stand up and approach the teacher. And Jaiswal went up to him wearing his rumpled shorts and hawai slippers, his white shirt that had become blue with ink stains.

The teacher looked at him and frowned. 'This will not do, Jaiswal. You have been selected for the interview. It is on Monday. The army people will be coming. Ask your mother to wash your shirt and shorts and iron them properly. You shall not come to the interview with these slippers. You will wear either white canvas shoes with white socks or black shoes, properly polished, with white socks. Is that understood?'

'Yes, sir,' Jaiswal replied.

Jaiswal told his parents that he had been selected for the interview. His father was a busy man. He often came home late from his shop, which was why he might not have paid much attention to what Jaiswal was saying. But his mother washed the school uniform twice over, grimly attacking the stubborn blues in the shirt that was once white.

There was no iron box at home. She kept the clothes folded under the pillow to smooth out the creases. The shoes were never bought. Jaiswal was petrified that if he turned up without the proper footwear, the mathematics teacher would give him a beating he would never forget. That night, as he slept, his mother came and woke him up to ask what the matter was – for he had been screaming in his sleep. He had had a nightmare about getting caned by Mahatham Singh.

Monday came around and Jaiswal still did not have the shoes he had been instructed to wear. He debated whether he should go at all, or feign illness, not so much because of the shoes, but the wrath he knew he would incur from his teacher. Then, thinking that giving the interview a miss would meet with worse results, he wore the uniform and reached the school in hawai slippers. There was a small building in the school called the Library, meant for the senior students. That was where the interviews were being conducted.

Mahatham Singh was right there waiting for them. He saw Jaiswal and called out to him. Then he lost his temper, while he gesticulated with his cane, shouting, 'Where are your shoes?'

Jaiswal started weeping and said, 'Guruji, I told my parents, but I could not get them.'

Seeing him cry, the mathematics teacher melted. 'Achcha, beta, don't cry. You do one thing. These slippers are very old and look very odd. When your turn comes for the interview, go in without your slippers. Go barefoot. At least your feet are clean. Should anybody ask you why you are barefoot, tell them that you have removed your shoes and left them outside out of respect for the elders and the fauj.'

When Jaiswal entered the room where the interview was being held, he saw the panel consisted of Wing Commander Mukherjee, who was the principal of Ghorakhal's Sainik School, and two other officers. All wore uniforms and looked very impressive. Jaiswal did a namaste and walked towards them. Immediately, they noticed that he had come inside without shoes and asked him why that was so. He responded as he had been coached. They began to laugh heartily.

A month later, Jaiswal was admitted to the Sainik School, but his father, when he saw the letter, immediately said the fee was too high and that he couldn't afford it. The boarding and lodging together came to Rs 200 per month. Later in the evening, though, he said there was a clause in the letter for those whose parents earned less than Rs 250 per month, and they could be considered for scholarship.

He furnished the declaration, and fifteen days later, Jaiswal's fees were waived. Then came another letter with a detailed list of clothing he had to take to the Sainik School.

The school sat in the Kumaon hills at a height of 6,000 feet, and from the parade ground you could see Bheemtal, with its houses far below, nestling in the slopes and the valleys, strewn around among trees that looked tiny. You could also see the roads winding up and down the hills, and in the distance Bheemtal lake that reflected the blue skies. In the winter, snow stood around in little clumps on the parade ground, like little soldiers.

David Kirkland had come from Coventry, England, as a voluntary teacher under the Volunteer Service Organisation (VSO) programme. He taught physics and mathematics. When Jaiswal was in class eight or nine, those were his favourite subjects. With Kirkland as his teacher, they became his obsessions.

Kirkland must have been in his early thirties. He was unpretentious and brisk. He always wore crumpled corduroy trousers and a T-shirt, which was often white in colour. On ceremonial occasions when all the staff and faculty turned up in pressed coats and ties, David Kirkland wore a tweed coat, but his tie hung loose, askew, below his collar, as if he was not comfortable with something holding him tightly by the throat. He wasn't married, and he lived in a room near the boy's hostel. He was always available in case the boys had doubts that needed to be cleared.

In his classes, Jaiswal knew the answers to all the tricky

questions Kirkland kept posing, and his hand would usually be the first to go up. Kirkland told the class one day, 'I have taught in England. I have taught in France. But I have not seen a brain like Anoop Jaiswal's.'

Jaiswal stood there, Kirkland's words burning into his brain, as Kirkland gave him a small toffee as a reward. It was wrapped in a pretty wrapper. It was a very small sweet, but to Jaiswal, it seemed a very significant and precious gift. He preserved it without eating it. The ants found it, and they didn't have to open the wrapper. They chewed their way through it. When he discovered the perforated wrapper many days later, there was nothing of the toffee left in it, not even a whiff that could be detected by his nose.

One time, Kirkland told Jaiswal, 'Why don't you think of becoming a scientist?' Was it one of his trick questions? Sometimes Jaiswal still thought of it that way, for he had started to want to become a scientist. That became his dream. He wanted to become a scientist. He was going to be a scientist! He was good at science, and even when he was in the ninth standard it hinged upon him to pull off the annual science exhibition, rather than the boys from the tenth or eleventh standard because his teacher supported Jaiswal, and he took it upon himself as a challenge as well.

One of the conditions of his joining Sainik School was that he had to sit for the National Defence Academy examinations. He had got a government scholarship, and since boarding, lodging and education were free, his father had to only pay a hundred rupees every year towards his schooling. Ten rupees every month was his pocket money.

His father had signed a bond to the effect that he would pay back the entire scholarship amount, in case Jaiswal didn't join the NDA. Jaiswal wanted to fail the exam so he could become a scientist. Instead, he passed because he was strong in mathematics. He went to the interview hoping to fail, but he passed again. At least his father was happy.

The village he belonged to, Mohra Samogar in Deoria district of western Uttar Pradesh, was dominated by Rajputs, or Kshatriyas. His father had inherited, from his father and his father before him, a double-barrelled twelve bore gun. That gun was Jaiswal's now.

In a Kshatriya-dominated community, a Vaishya possessing a double-barrelled gun was unusual. Whenever they went to his father's village, Jaiswal would be the one assigned to carry the gun. In the evenings, they went to the riverbank to shoot wild birds which flocked there. Jaiswal was amazed how his father was able to bring down three or four birds in one shot. At that time, he didn't know it was loaded with buckshot – forty or fifty pellets fanned out in a wide arc to hit the birds every time the gun was fired. The birds in the middle of the arc had very little chance of survival.

Very few people in the army were from the business community, the Vaishyas. The highest rank of any person in Jaiswal's father's village was subedar major. Such was the achievement that whenever the subedar major came back home on leave, he would always come in uniform, full regalia, shoes, epaulets, cap, regimental colours, and with his entire quota of Old Monk rum, which he had saved up during his service period. It was a big deal when people gathered to listen to his tales and drink the army rum.

When Jaiswal made it into the air force as a cadet, he was on the flight path to becoming a class one gazetted officer. He could sign with green ink. Mohra Samogar was stunned. His father invited all the people from the village for a banquet of bedmi, biriyani, peta and kurchan.

Men from the other Kshatriya families were also there. Some of their children had joined the police, mostly as constables. Nobody in Mohra Samogar had reached the level of a sub-inspector yet. But even being a constable – wearing a uniform, going around on a Bullet motorcycle, carrying arms – was a big deal.

At the dinner, a person belonging to a Kshatriya family remarked, 'It is the sign of Kaliyug that a Vaishya's son is going to become a fighter pilot, flying fighter planes, while the Kshatriya's sons are hunting for jobs.' He emphasized the word 'fighter' more than the word 'pilot'. Jaiswal's father – he did not know what got into him – shot back, 'Aaj kal ki ladayi mein bhi padhai ki zaroorat hoti hai!' (You cannot fight today's war without education.) His father added, 'I see the Kshatriyas are carrying arms and doing sword practice, but where is the education in that?'

At Khadakvasla, Jaiswal felt stifled, crushed. It was more rigorous than the Sainik School life. He was not even fifteen days into the NDA when the worst thing happened. In the science class, an officer from the army education corps was teaching physics. He wrote out a problem on the board to be solved, thinking that it was a difficult problem.

The problem was a long one, and it dealt with conservation of momentum. The answer to the question was in inverse proportion to the question, a simple one-line answer, keeping conservation of energy also in mind. Jaiswal could see where the question was going, even as the teacher wrote it out from one end of the long blackboard to the other, the chalk squeaking with excitement. Jaiswal had the answer in a jiffy. He wrote it in his notebook and went to show it to him. The teacher took the notebook and looked at the answer and how he got it and frowned, and then said, 'Don't do it like this. Solve it this way. You have done it the wrong way. This is the right way.'

Jaiswal said, 'But this is the right way, sir. The answer is right.'

'No, I am not interested in your answer.'

Jaiswal insisted that he was right, and the teacher kept saying Jaiswal was wrong.

'Cadet Anoop Jaiswal, stop being insolent and stand on that chair!'

'Sir, I am not insolent!'

'There you go again. You are answering back! Stand on that chair!'

'But, sir, I am right! Why should I be punished for that?'

According to the teacher, Jaiswal had talked back, not once but twice. For that, not only did he have to stand on the chair, he was given ten days' restriction – which meant that while all the other cadets played football or hockey, Jaiswal had to practise parading and running in the evening, for two whole hours.

He was aghast that a disagreement in physics class could turn into a punishment. He was in turmoil that night, and the next day he told the authorities in the NDA that he wanted to leave and wouldn't continue.

They told him that he was a minor. Unless his father gave them an application in writing, he could not leave. Jaiswal wrote a panicked letter to his father that morning, begging him to please let him come back home; he didn't want to continue in the NDA. In the afternoon, he wrote another letter to his father with the words, 'Please take me back.' In the evening, he wrote yet another letter to him, filled with the same entreaties and emotional appeals.

For two days, they kept threatening him that all the fees would have to be paid back before he could leave the NDA. It was the longest two days of his life. His father read the three letters and finally came to take him away. He didn't utter a word, but as they left, rested his hand on Jaiswal's shoulder.

The NDA was insisting that the money be paid back, the money the government had spent on educating Jaiswal. But his father didn't have sufficient funds for that. He consulted a lawyer who advised him to reply to the authorities, saying that the bond obligation had ended when his son had written and passed the NDA examination, cleared the interview and had consequently been admitted into the NDA. That was all he had pledged, that he would be obligated to send his son to the NDA. Once he was enrolled in the NDA, his obligation ended, and thereafter he had no further compulsion as per his bond. After joining, if his son left, the father was not liable, and no clause in his bond held him to any further obligation. He attached a copy of the bond and sent it off. He didn't hear from the authorities again.

Jaiswal then enrolled in Delhi University to pursue an honours course in physics.

Jaiswal's father was a very affectionate person, particularly to him. The wealth of affection that was showered on him in his childhood, and even afterwards, far overshadowed the paucities that the family had to face. When he thought back on their lives then, he realized his father must have barely scraped through from month to month. Jaiswal had not known that when he was young.

Before he went to Sainik School at Ghorakhal, he had been selected for the Rashtriya Indian Military College at Dehradun. His father had argued against him joining there. Only later did Jaiswal realize that his father couldn't afford the fees. He simply wouldn't have been able to pay the money.

His father's income, in the late sixties, while Jaiswal was still in school, couldn't have been more than Rs 250 per month. He had lost his father by the age of five, and had been brought up in a joint family by his uncles. He had had his own share of difficulties and had married very late. By the time Jaiswal was in college doing his MSc, his father was already about sixty-six years of age. Only then had it dawned on Jaiswal that his father's business – he dealt with hardware and building materials in Gorakhpur – was not going very well.

Jaiswal's elder brother, who was already married, had a family of his own, which was dependent on that business as well. His father never told Jaiswal openly of his dire financial situation. Sometimes, he asked how much more time he would take to complete his PhD and research and all that. Jaiswal could never give him a satisfactory answer. He himself did not know. But he realized that it was high time that he began to earn his own living.

It helped that by the time he finished his MSc Jaiswal had become highly disillusioned with science as a subject. The passion that had once been ignited by David Kirkland was comprehensively doused by the professors of Delhi University. The conversations in the corridors and the faculty rooms of the university were about the kind of jobs they were likely to get, the pay and the perks that would come with them, or how they could get out of the country and go to some foreign country where they could become scientists. Many professors advised that if science or academics were to be chosen as a career, the students should shun subjects like general theory of relativity or quantum mechanics, as those were theoretical subjects, which very few colleges or universities encouraged.

It was better to embrace engineering, which had straightforward technological and practical applications. Like a pincer, this dull and aching reality caught Jaiswal and effectively crushed his dream of becoming a scientist. He felt a compulsion to find a job.

By that time, he had met Neelam. Neelam, his wife, had been his classmate in the physics honours course at Hindu College in Delhi University. He had known her for nearly five years before they were married. Mutual attraction was immediate, though they were opposites in their approach to academics. She was meticulous, very conscious of the syllabus, and paid attention to what was taught in the classroom. She often told Jaiswal that he was only a dreamer who did not see the realities of life. Jaiswal never paid attention to the syllabus and studied whatever he liked. The number of classes he bunked was more than the ones he attended.

To marry her, however, he needed to find a job. He couldn't make her wait indefinitely. They belonged to completely different stratas of society, community and caste. Her parents were Derawals, a closely knit community that had migrated from the Pakistan–Afghanistan border during Partition. Her father was an officer in Indian Oil, and most of her relatives were in government service.

Jaiswal sat for various examinations, including the ones related to banking. Both he and Neelam became probationary officers – Jaiswal in the State Bank of India in Azamgarh, Uttar Pradesh, and Neelam in Andhra Bank, Delhi. She was posted to the Karol Bagh branch, near the place where her parents stayed. Their jobs made the marriage possible. Jaiswal continued to take various examinations, including the civil services examination, where he opted for mathematics as the main subject. He was selected for the Indian Police Service.

At times, a thought would ripple through, somewhere in the back of his head – if he was fated to wear a uniform, then it should have been the air force uniform. He didn't want to become a police officer.

His first brush with the police had left him with an unpleasant memory. In 1971, he had been in the tenth standard. From school, a batch of sixty-five boys, and about seven teachers, went to Ootacamund (now Udhagamandalam). An all-India camp of Sainik School boys was being held there. From Nainital, they came down the hill on a bus to Mathura, where two special railway bogies, one a three-tier bogey and the other a first-class one, were to take them south. The first-class bogie was meant for officers and teachers; the three-tier compartment had seventy-two berths and the students were sixty-five in number, so they had the whole bogie to themselves. The bogies were attached to various trains as they travelled deeper south. Forty-eight hours later, early in the morning, they arrived in Madras.

The train to Coimbatore, from where they had to change trains to go up the Nilgiris, was in the evening. They had the whole day to themselves. The practice was they would take their luggage out on the platform and take turns guarding it while they waited for their coaches to get shunted to the next train. The guard duty changed every three hours.

Having piled their luggage on the platform, Jaiswal, along with four friends, Subash Chandra Rai, R.P. Sahi, and two others, decided to go and see the sea. They had never seen the sea before. They knew there was a beach in Madras, and at the railway platform when they asked the way to it, they were told it was nearby, within walking distance. Every few minutes they would ask for directions and every few minutes they were told the sea was nearby.

They reached Anna Samadhi – the memorial dedicated to C.N. Annadurai. And the sea was right there. Jaiswal and his friends walked the breadth of the beach from Anna Samadhi. He even measured the steps – it was half a kilometre of sand. He took off his chappals on the beach, his feet sinking into the warm sand. The sea stretched as far as he could see, glittering, the crests of the waves wearing foam as wave after wave roared to the shore. The noise! There was not a cloud in the sky. Jaiswal had never seen or heard anything like it. It was around half past nine in the morning in the month of June. The sea glinted so harshly it hurt the eyes.

They wanted to enter the water. So they removed their clothes, down to their briefs; they weighted their clothes with footwear, placing them in the shadow of the big fishing boats, the giant catamarans that had pulled up above the waterline and ran smack into the water. The salt water was unpleasant, and the waves pummelled them. After about fifteen minutes of frolicking, they gave up. There was too much heat, salt, too much effort to counter the waves.

They came out, dried themselves, and sat in the shadow of the big catamarans. Near the Anna Samadhi, there were some trees. They wound their way back to that area and rested in the shade. A few minutes had passed when one of them eagerly pulled out a pack of cards from his pocket. They could play a game!

Suddenly, a couple of policemen were standing over them. Their shadows fell diagonally across the sunlit patch where the boys sat. A third policeman joined them. They were all wearing khaki shorts.

One of them pointed to the cards and said something in Tamil. The boys immediately stood up. One of the policemen seized the cards. The boys tried to tell the police they were not gambling, but they didn't seem interested in what they were saying. Come to the police station, they kept repeating. They had no choice but to go along.

The prospect of going inside a police station frightened them. Maybe playing cards was a crime. Would they be sent to jail from the police station? They had grown up in an isolated hostel, going home only briefly for holidays. They didn't have any knowledge of the police. Neither had they informed their teachers that they were going to the beach. The headmaster was a very strict man, a squadron leader, and he had accompanied them on the train.

Now their parents would be informed.

They panicked and began to plead with the policemen. One policeman checked their pockets. They were looking for money. The boys would receive five rupees every day as ration money while they were travelling. Every morning, a teacher would come and hand over five rupees to each of them and they signed on the ledger that the teacher brought along, acknowledging they had received the amount. The boys had to manage food and anything else with that. The five rupees covered breakfast, lunch and dinner. It was an adequate amount.

That day, the maximum that came out of their pockets, when the policemen made them turn out their pockets, were five rupees in total. Most had a rupee or a couple of rupees and some change. One of the policemen collected the money, and again they were made to walk with the policemen to the police station. They had almost reached the wide road that fronts Marina Beach. The boys talked among themselves in Hindi. Rai said, 'Let us run away at the count of three, and he started to count, ek, do, teen…'

They fled, ran as fast as they could, but the policemen came behind them, running as well. There were two of them, and they were gaining up on the boys. Running with slippers was proving difficult, and Rai said, 'Chappal phek do, aur tej bhago!' (Do away with your slippers and run fast!) They threw their slippers away and ran even faster. They ran for their lives. Over the Napier Bridge, with the gleaming white spans of its wide footpath, the Cooum river was darkly still below them and the sun blazing over them. Only when they crossed the Napier Bridge did they stop to check where the policemen were. They were struggling now, with their boots on, and had fallen behind, but the boys kept running, covered in sweat, till they reached the central station. All they wanted to do was merge into the crowds. And drink water, lots of water.

During the Emergency, Jaiswal was in Delhi University and the campus would swirl with stories of illegal arrests and police atrocities. Many of the professors had been hauled up, and the hostel warden constantly warned the students not to argue, not to speak loudly; he didn't want the police coming into the campus and taking students away.

Jaiswal had a very negative image of the civil service. He thought they had sold out during the Emergency, and even before Independence, all the bureaucrats ever did was be guided by imperialist impulses, as if they were second-hand white-skinned people. They served the Crown more than the country; the police was just a dirty arm of the British colonial government. It was strange to think that he was going to be a police officer, maybe even a director general of police one day.

Nevertheless, Jaiswal signed up for the Indian Police Service. It was 1980. There were more drills and parades and outdoor activities, which proved to not be an issue, Jaiswal having been in Sainik School. He did well. However, in the classroom where senior officers came and gave lectures, it was another matter. Any questioning, any disagreements, were frowned upon and taken adversely. The subtext was that wisdom came only with hierarchy. Accordingly, the director of the academy was the wisest. The director knew everything. And if he told them something, they were supposed to listen with mouths tightly shut. They were finely tuned, it seemed to him in retrospect, to sniff out aberrations that entered the portals of the National Police Academy at Hyderabad. The director himself was fond of taking classes at the academy. His relentless enthusiasm drove him. Sometimes he taught law, though another teacher was formally assigned for this subject. They were all new to law. The police probationers sat like sheep in the director's class.

B.K. Roy, the director, was teaching two sections of the Indian Penal Code – Section 379, simple theft. If you stole something from a person, a watch, car, cycle, or something, it amounted to a simple theft. This was punishable with an imprisonment of up to three years. The next section was 380, which dealt with theft from a tent, building or vessel. If you entered a building and stole something, for example, from inside the building, you could be punished with imprisonment up to seven years.

Jaiswal thought about this and then raised his hand. The director looked at him quizzically but gave him permission to proceed.

'Sir, there seems to be a contradiction in these sections.'

'Contradiction, eh?' The director looked alarmed. 'What contradiction?' He peered at Jaiswal through his oversized thick black-framed spectacles, pursing his thin lips.

'Suppose, sir, there is a boat in the harbour. . .'

'Well, get on with it.'

'Sir, if I enter the boat and take away a transistor lying in the boat, sir, it amounts to a theft from a vessel. And under Section 380, I will be liable for imprisonment up to seven years, correct?'

'What are you getting at?'

'Sir, what if I entered the boat and took away the boat, along with the transistor? That would be theft of a vessel and not from a vessel and hence, according to Section 379, I will be given imprisonment of only up to three years?'

For a moment, the director did not say anything. Then he carefully asked, 'Are you making a joke? You want to make fun?'

'No, sir. It is a genuine doubt.'

'You want to make fun of everything, eh? You think you know the law better than others?'

'No, sir. I do not know anything about the law, which is why I am asking.'

'Are you being sarcastic?'

'No, sir. While you were teaching, this doubt flashed in my mind, that's all.'

'Why should it flash only in your mind? So many other cadets are sitting here and listening to me. It has not flashed in their minds, has it?' He looked around the classroom and asked, 'Has this flashed in any of your esteemed minds, eh?'

A fog of silence enveloped his query. Then he stared at Jaiswal.

'You are the only genius in class, eh? I have been hearing reports about you. I have been hearing not very nice reports about you. Adverse reports, in fact. You want to make fun of everything and everybody, eh?'

It should have struck Jaiswal then that he had made an adverse impression on the senior staff simply by being curious. His teachers in the Academy were no David Kirklands, not by a long shot.

It was the month of June. At half past six in the morning, the cadets would go for physical training. They usually woke up at five in the morning got ready and were in the lobby by six fifteen. There were fifty cadets and had to fall into squads. There were four squads of about twelve cadets each. They would then be made to march in the parade ground for PT, or physical training.

That day when they gathered in the lobby, it was pouring. There was some talk as to where the parade would be held – In the auditorium? Or in the field? As it was being debated, a trainer ran up holding an umbrella over his head, while blowing a whistle and shouting, 'Run to the field for PT! Run to the field for parade!'

Some cadet shouted, 'Send us a bus. It is raining!' They remained in the lobby until the rain came down to a drizzle and they could hear the whistle being blown again and again insistently. They ran to the field. Jaiswal was one of the first few to reach the ground and report for the parade.

All of them were issued memos. All fifty, asking why they were late for the parade. Orders had been given, and those orders had been disobeyed. Being late was being viewed as insubordination.

Jaiswal was singled out, and was told that not only had he come late for the parade, but he had had instigated others not to go to the parade also.

In his reply, Jaiswal wrote, 'Dear sir, as far as my being late for PT by ten minutes, I sincerely regret the lapse. But the other charge that I instigated the others to be late is baseless, without a single iota of truth. I request the authorities to have a thorough enquiry into such an allegation because I have never had such a plebeian mentality.'

The director summoned each cadet into his room individually, and each one of them was made to say 'I apologize for being late'. The director went through that with all of the forty-nine cadets, one after the other.

Jaiswal was the last to be called in. When it was his turn, the director turned a baleful eye on Jaiswal and burst out, 'You! You talk a lot! Can't you apologize?'

'Sir, I have apologized in my written reply.'

'No, no. You only said you regret the lapse. That is not an apology, and that too, after you instigated the whole lot.'

'No, sir, that is wrong. I will never agree with it. I will never apologize for it.'

'You are talking back!'

'No, sir. We get up at five in the morning, and we are on the parade ground soon thereafter. Where is the time to instigate others and why should others get instigated?'

'This is what we hate about you. You talk back. You are insolent.'

'Sir, think of what you are asking. You are asking me to apologize for something I have not done.'

The director stared at Jaiswal for a long time and then abruptly spat out the word, 'Go!'

Jaiswal saluted him and went out. The matter ended. Or so he thought. The training continued. They were a happy lot. In August, all got their cadres. Jaiswal was allotted Tamil

Nadu. There was some talk that he would be judged the best cadet for outdoor. It was time to move out of the Academy. It was the end of November. Fifteen days before the passing out parade, they began doing practice parades. Usually, after the parade practice, there was some respite. Jaiswal was resting in his room when there was a knock on his door. 'Who is it?' he asked.

The postman said, 'There is a letter for you. Registered letter.'

Jaiswal signed for it and opened the envelope. It said, 'The Government of India is pleased to discharge you from service under the orders of the President of India.'

Jaiswal didn't know what to make of this. Was it standard for those who finished the training? He knocked on the door of the next cadet and asked, did he receive a letter like this, but he had not. He knocked on each batchmate's door and no one had received this letter, not one of them. Jaiswal went to the office building, showed the superintendent the letter. He looked at the letter and looked at Jaiswal and said, 'Get a good lawyer and fight it. They have removed you from service.'

There was a deputy director, Mr Luthra. Jaiswal entered his room in a daze, and asked him, 'What is happening, sir? What kind of punishment is this? And for what, sir?'

'No, Jaiswal. This is not a punishment. He paused before he chose his words. It is just ... how do I say this ... it is just that you are not suitable for police service. It is not good for you to continue in a service where you are not suitable. It suits neither you nor the police.'

He patted him on his shoulder. 'You are young. You will find another job. I am sure.'

'But sir, what is the reason?'

'It happens sometimes, Jaiswal.'

'But I am told this has never happened.'

Behind him, there was a big board. It said Satyam Eva Jayate. Jaiswal pointed at it, and the deputy director turned and saw the board.

'Sir,' Jaiswal asked, 'does this board hold any meaning for you?'

He didn't say anything. Jaiswal went away.

He went to the director's office and sought an appointment. His PA said he would tell the director and let Jaiswal know. Jaiswal went back to his room and began to pack his belongings. The Hindi teacher, Pandeyji, came to his room in the evening and told him that the director had asked him to go to his residence at alf past six in the evening for a cup of tea, not to his office. By six twenty, Jaiswal was at the director's residence. He asked the orderly if the director was in, but apparently he wasn't, he was told. Inside, the lights were burning bright, as if festivities were about to start. He paced outside the director's official residence for over an hour. At half past seven in the evening he asked the orderly again and again he said, no, the director had not come back.

Jaiswal turned back to return to his room. As he was walking back, he met Pandeyji on the way and told him, 'Director saab toh nahin aye.' (The director was still not at home.)

Pandeyji said, 'No, I was with him. Wait, wait, he is coming. He is feeling very bad. Actually, mujhse poocha (he asked me) how to face the boy now?'

Apparently the civil trainers had been arguing with the director over what had happened. Nobody had ever found fault with Jaiswal. There were what was called guide officer meetings. Five cadet officers were put under the supervision of one senior officer, and every fifteen days the guide officer met his wards and in those meetings they would be constantly giving feedback on their training and performance and learning, telling the wards to concentrate on this, to improve on this. Justice Banerji, who was a district judge, was Jaiswal's guide officer. In not a single one of those interactions had a word been spoken or deficiency mentioned.

Jaiswal went back to the director's residence and waited again. The director came a little later and made him sit down and offered him a glass of lemonade, and asked, 'Jaiswal, who was against you in this academy?'

'I don't know. All of you, my teachers, are my father's age. I can't think of anybody being against me.'

He said, 'Look, I am writing to the Government of India. It happened in the heat of the moment. We realize we have judged you very harshly. I am requesting the Government of India to revoke the order. If you can go to Delhi quickly, to the Ministry of Home Affairs, see that they act on my letter revoking the order. I will be sending the letter directly, but I will give you a copy of it to keep with you and to take to the MHA.'

The deputy director, who was there with him, intervened and said, 'That won't be necessary, sir, to give him the copy of the letter. We should send it directly.'

The director agreed with him but instructed that the letter be read out to Jaiswal.

The following day, Jaiswal left for Delhi. His father-in-law's cousin, P.K. Kathpalia was the additional secretary, Home. He met him and his father-in-law also talked to him, but nothing happened. He wanted to meet the home secretary, T.N. Chaturvedi, but had no luck.

Jaiswal hung around Chaturvedi's office in North Block. Those days, there was no security in the way there is now. He heard that the home secretary had arrived in the room, and so he went inside without being ushered in. He did not have an appointment. Jaiswal introduced himself, apprised him of his situation and told him the director had written a letter explaining the mistake. Chaturvedi barely looked at him, didn't ask him to sit down.

The home secretary was brusque. He said, 'If there is a mistake, someone has to go. One of you has to go. Either you. Or the director. The guilty should go.'

Jaiswal tried to speak. The home secretary cut him short and pressed the bell, calling his PA.

'No, I can make out. I see clearly. You are not fit to be an officer. How can you come in here without an appointment? Is that an officer-like thing to do?'

'Sir, I have been trying for almost three days. I have been waiting here to meet you.'

'No, no. You are unfit.'

'In that case, sir, I will be left with no other option but to go to the court,' Jaiswal blurted it out, without thinking.

Chaturvedi stood up, furious, and he banged his desk as he said it, 'My boy, nothing on this earth will bring you back to the job or this career! Do you hear? Nothing!'

The PA had run into the room and was standing there, cowering.

'If there is justice, I will be back, sir. If there is no justice, I will not want to come back. I came to you because you are the highest authority in the department. If things are like this today, it is likely to continue like this. If there is no justice then I do not want to come back. Nothing will make me. I would not want to serve in a place where things are so arbitrary.'

As Jaiswal left, he could hear the home secretary berating the PA for having people loitering around the room. 'What is this? Is this a public convenience that anybody can walk in and out at will?'

On 25 November Jaiswal reached Gorakhpur, his father's home. He had to think of a way ahead. But first, he had to tell his father. There was a complication. His sister was to be married on 29 November. He had applied for leave, but it had been rejected. He hadn't told his parents that it had been turned down. Having been dismissed, there was no need now to tell them. They thought that his leave must have been approved, and that he must have come to attend the marriage. He did not want to cast a shadow of gloom on the festivities.

After his sister had left home with her groom, when his father was more relaxed, and taking stock of the expenses of the marriage, Jaiswal sat near him and told him what had happened. He could see that his father was stunned, although he did not say much. He had faith in his son's sincerity. Both sat in silence, his father with his account book open and his pen resting on it. Then he got up, pulled his shirt from the rope that ran across the room from one side to the other, where his towel, his banian and his washed clothes were hanging. He, then, opened his almirah, pulled out a bundle of papers and asked Jaiswal to accompany him. They got into a rickshaw. Jaiswal asked him where they were going. They were going to meet Panditji, the principal of the Sanskrit Rawat Pathshala.

Panditji was also a renowned astrologer. He knew his father well, and as his father sat before him, Panditji saw Jaiswal and smiled and asked how he was doing. His father gave Panditji the papers he had brought along. It was Jaiswal's horoscope. Panditji opened it and pored over it for a while. Then he looked at Jaiswal's father and said, 'Oh! Very dark clouds have come upon your son now.'

'Is there a remedy?' his father asked. Panditji scrutinized the horoscope again, wordlessly. Then he said, 'The clouds will be there for two years. There is nothing you can do about it. Thereafter, the sun will tear through the clouds and smile.'

Jaiswal's father made a wry face, and told Panditji, 'But Panditji, my son has already been dismissed from the academy. So where is the question of the sun smiling?'

'I don't know the ways of God. The ways of God are different. I am telling you what your son's horoscope is saying. For two years, he has to suffer.'

Jaiswal went to the Delhi High Court. This was sometime in 1982. The court had to decide whether the case could even be admitted. In 1983 it came up before Justice Talwar of the Delhi High Court. When the case was called out, the government pleader got up.

The judge got worked up when he heard what the government pleader said. 'Don't waste the court's time,' he said. 'He is a probationer. He was found unsuitable. He was thrown out. It is good that such persons are weeded out. What can this court do about this? It is because of us judges that there is so much indiscipline in the police force. If he can prove malice, then, yes, he might have something. But I am not entertaining this.'

He flung away the file. It was so shocking that Jaiswal's lawyer didn't meet him outside the courtroom. Crestfallen, he walked all the way from the high court near India Gate to Pusa Road, where Neelam's parents lived in a small apartment on the second floor. Her parents were pained by the dismissal. Neelam had quit her job when their son, Manu, was born, a development her parents were unhappy with as they had repeatedly told her not to quit her bank job.

Neelam had her reasons, though. She had found that as a bank officer, she could not be with her husband for long; her postings were different from her husband's, whose cadre was Tamil Nadu. To their bad luck, her resignation from the bank was accepted in the month of October 1981. A month later Jaiswal was dismissed from service in November 1981. They now had a son to look after and no source of income.

It was then that her father advised her that it would be prudent if she moved to Delhi. With her qualification of MPhil and BEd, it would be easier for her to get a teaching assignment in some good school or college in the capital. They told her that at least till the time Jaiswal was reinstated in service or found some other job, she should remain in Delhi. It was practical advice, but her contention was different. She told her parents she could not leave her husband while he was without a job. She stayed in Gorakhpur.

Jaiswal began staying in her parents' flat in a busy area on Pusa Road whenever there was a hearing. His father-in-law was a worldly man with strong views. To him, it was clear that if you wanted to serve in any organization, compromises would have to be made. Senior officers should be given proper respect, even if they were somewhat whimsical. Jaiswal's in-laws felt that he had a weak case and hence would not win. They found his arguments philosophical. No judge would buy them, they felt. With what face would he meet them now?

When Jaiswal reached Neelam's father's home from the high court and told them what had happened, his mother-in-law remarked that she was not at all surprised by this turn of events. 'The courts would not help you,' she told her son-in-law emphatically. It was three days later that Jaiswal summoned the courage to meet his lawyer again.

To make matters worse, on the heels of the Delhi High Court incident, the new director who succeeded Roy at the Police Academy in Hyderabad gave a press conference, making Jaiswal seem as a rebellious sort of person; that Jaiswal came from a very well-to-do family and that he had joined the IPS just for the heck of it. The new director added that it was feared Jaiswal had extremist links. It was all published in the local press and someone brought them to Jaiswal's notice. He collected all the cuttings, and with the help of a very junior lawyer, they filed a Special Leave Petition (SLP).

The *Sunday* magazine, which was published out of Calcutta, carried a two-page article on it. *India Today*, which was then a fortnightly, carried a small article. The local press was full of it. On 30 August 1983, the SLP was immediately admitted but by a very difficult bench – a two-judge bench by Chandrachud, who was the Chief Justice, and Venkataramiah, who would go on to become Chief Justice.

Those days Jaiswal used to travel very often between Delhi and Gorakhpur to pursue the case. Either the hearing would get postponed, or a date would be given but the matter would not come up for hearing. It would be listed, but when he reached, some previous case would take up the time and his hearing would get deferred.

Once he was returning to Gorakhpur by the Gomti Express. The train, a chair class, would take eight hours to reach the destination. On either side of the aisle, three people could sit on wooden benches. It was a fast train. Only two halts between Delhi and Gorakhpur, which were Aligarh and Lucknow.

On that day, five people of one group were sitting on one group of chairs and Jaiswal was the sixth. He had a window seat. One of the people in the group was reading the *Sunday* magazine that had published the Hyderabad story. He said, 'Dekhiye, aise aise goonde badmash bhi IPS ho jaate hain. Yeh Jaiswal to Dilli University ka maana hua goonda tha. Baat baat me chakku nikaal leta ...' (See how thugs such as Jaiswal also become IPS officers. Jaiswal was a notorious hooligan at Delhi University, known for flashing his knife at every opportunity ...)

The magazine had mentioned that Jaiswal had studied in Delhi University. It was strange to hear them speak of him in front of him, and he didn't recognize any of them. Neither did he recognize himself in the conversation. He couldn't help but intervene.

'Bhaiyya, aap Anoop Jaiswal ko jaante hain kya?' (Brother, do you know Jaiswal?) he asked.

'Haan. Main Dilli University mein padha tha. Woh toh maana hua goonda tha!' (Yes, I studied in Delhi University, and he used to be an infamous hooligan there.)

'Aapne dekha hai usse kabhi?' (Have you ever seen him?)

'Haan. Main bohauth baar dekh chuka hoon. Bohauth badmash aadmi hai woh. Kafi bura reputation tha uska. Pata nahin kaise IPS ho gaya woh.' (Yes, I used to see him quite often. He was known as a bad character with a bad reputation. Wonder how he became IPS.)

'Nahin, sir, aapne dekha nahin hoga is Anoop Jaiswal ko. Aise hi bol rahein hain aap.' (No, sir. I don't think you have seen him. You are bad-mouthing him without reason.)

The magazine-reader's friend then intervened. 'Aap in par shak kyon kar rahein hain?' (Why do you doubt what my friend is saying?)

'Kyunki Anoop Jaiswal main hoon. Aur main goonda nahin hoon.' (Because I am Anoop Jaiswal, and I am no ruffian or thug.)

Then one of them said, 'Nahin, nahin. Woh koi aur hoga, confuse kar rahein hain naam ko.' (Our friend might have been confused and is referring to someone else.)

Jaiswal kept quiet for the rest of the journey.

When the matter came up in the Supreme Court in September that year, 1983, the government lawyer was asked, 'Isn't it the case where someone was dismissed for not attending a yoga class?'

The government lawyer immediately said, 'Your Honour, all press reports are incorrect.'

Jaiswal had mentioned in the SLP that the characterization that had been given by the director of the academy, who had been quoted in the reports, was absurd.

The bench asked Jaiswal, 'So what are you doing now?'

'Who will give me a job with such serious allegations against me, Your Honour? Who will give me a job when I am being falsely painted and my name besmirched, Your Honour?'

The judge asked the government lawyer, 'If the reports

are untrue and you are declaring it as such, did you publish a denial?'

The government lawyer did not say anything.

'Did you or did you not publish a denial?'

'We will come back on that, Your Honour,' the government lawyer said.

In the counter affidavit filed by the government, they had committed a major error. They had written that Jaiswal had been dismissed from the Indian Air Force but had not revealed this fact to the Union Public Service Commission or to the Government of India. In his rejoinder, Jaiswal had stated that this was a totally and blatantly false allegation and that he had never been dismissed. He had resigned on his own within twenty days of joining. The records in Air Headquarters and the National Defence Academy would reflect that.

The court pointed this out to the lawyer. 'How can you say dismissed? He says he resigned. Dismissal and resignation are two different things. We want to see the records for this. Are you trying to confuse the court?'

The government lawyer said he would come back on this point as well.

According to the law in those days, the appointing authority had the power to discharge any probationer, applicable to all services, without assigning any suitable reasons. Once you signed up, and you were under training, you were being judged. Jaiswal built the argument in his affidavit that discharging a person without assigning reason was one thing. But discharging a person without reason was another. Even if you did not assign a reason, the reason should exist somewhere in the file, tangibly and verifiably.

The judges asked, 'How do you prove that it was without reason?'

Jaiswal said every fifteen days the guide officer met him and four other probationers in his room to review the progress that had been made in the previous fortnight. Never had there been an exchange of paper or even a word in the form of advice or caution between Jaiswal and the authority. No warning that he was not meeting the required standards or that he was weak in any subject. Jaiswal argued that it was not possible, therefore, to become unsuitable overnight. Unsuitability had to be noticed over a period and a chance given to make a suitable effort to overcome it. The law ought not to be implemented in a manner that defeated the very purpose for which it was created.

There was one other charge that had been made. It was regarding the leaves Jaiswal had been permitted to take while in the academy. He had been given two days' leave to see his wife in the month of February. She had undergone a caesarean operation. The leave period was a Saturday and Sunday, the weekend. He left on Friday and Monday morning was the day he had to report back. Jaiswal had made arrangements to arrive at the Secunderabad station at seven in the morning on Monday.

The Academy at Shivaramapalli was an hour away by taxi. On the way back, at Kazipet, about one hundred and forty kilometres away, his train was derailed, and luckily he wasn't injured. But consequently, Jaiswal arrived only in the afternoon. An explanation was sought, and he said there was a derailment that delayed him, but he had attended the classes that afternoon. He was marked half-day leave without pay and they deducted his salary accordingly. In his affidavit, Jaiswal had stated the matter was settled: he had been delayed but the explanation had been accepted. He had been given a half-day leave without pay and salary was deducted accordingly. Jaiswal argued malice. The judge went through the affidavit and asked the government lawyer, 'Where is the charge in this? The matter is settled. Where is the charge here?'

The bench then said, 'We will look into this matter. In the meantime, why can't this man complete his training and rejoin the academy? We will give a stay on the dismissal.'

At that time, Jaiswal asked his lawyer how long this process could take. The judge saw him talking to the lawyer and asked, 'What is the matter?'

'Your Honour,' Jaiswal stood up and said, 'one dismissal is bad enough, but two will be disastrous.'

'What do you mean, two dismissals?'

'If I lose the case again, I will be dismissed again, milord.'

Justice Venkataramiah looked amused. 'What do you want, then?'

'Milord, if I have to serve society as a police officer, my youth should not be wasted waiting for a judgement. If I serve, I serve now, Your Honour. It is either now or never.'

Justice Venkataramiah smiled and said, 'A very reasonable request! No stay granted. But the matter shall be disposed of, within twelve weeks from today. And as he is not working, he shall be exempted from all court fees and the like.' Twelve weeks meant that it would be December that year.

The government pleader got up and suggested that there should be a notice. 'There is no need for notice,' the judge noted. 'You just bring the file. There is no argument in this. If he is unsuitable, the reason for it will be there on the file. You just bring it. The matter ends there.'

The government pleader was a Sikh, a recently retired former Chief Justice of the Sikkim High Court, Manmohan Singh Gujral. After twelve weeks, when the records were to be brought, the case came before the two-judge bench of Justice E.S. Venkataramiah and Justice R.B. Misra. The government pleader got up and said he wanted fifteen more days to produce the file because the file was not traceable.

Justice Venkataramiah addressed the government pleader, 'Oh, so you know that this bench is not going to sit for more than a week. So, you are not happy with this bench? Let a senior officer from the Ministry of Home Affairs, which is a stone's throw from us, come and depose before us that the file is missing and we will meet at two today.'

Somehow, the file managed to find its way to the court before 2 p.m. that afternoon. At the court, Justice Venkataramiah held up the file and waved it at Manmohan Singh Gujral. 'Now you know why the file was missing, don't you? There is nothing inside it. It is empty!'

Gujral said, 'No, Your Honour. It is not about what Mr Jaiswal did or did not do. It is the attitude.' He contended before the judge that Jaiswal was basically of a defiant nature.

They pointed to a matter of 1893 where an ICS officer had been discharged from service for an 'unsuitable attitude'. The ICS officer had declared in a speech somewhere that England could not have true democracy so long as it held colonies elsewhere because democracy was a matter of spirit. By holding colonies, it showed that England was not democracy-minded. England did not consider everyone equal. When such was the reality, England could not have true democracy even in its own homeland. For holding and espousing such thoughts, the ICS officer was removed from service.

When Gujral had finished his expostulation, Justice Venkataramiah remarked, 'It was the bad luck of this ICS officer that we did not exist then. Mr Gujral, do you think the values espoused by the rulers of colonial India should also be held aloft in a democratic and free India?'

Jaiswal had made the argument that in the name of discipline what was really being demanded was servility. He was ready to be disciplined but was not ready to be servile.

The judge told the government pleader, 'You are a Sardarji and you may not follow this, but in UP and Bihar there exists a common practice of touching a big man's feet when you go to him for some favour. By touching his feet, it is not ensured that your work will be done. But if you fail to touch his feet, then it is ensured that your work will never be done. Do you think that the Supreme Court should take into consideration such things?'

They reserved the judgement for a day. The next day, the operative portion of the judgement was read out.

As Anoop Jaiswal stood before the judges, the bench said, 'Look, the government took away your job. It is the Constitution of India and the law of the land which is restoring it back to you. It is a lease given by the law to you. We hope you live up to that lease. Your loyalty shall ever remain to the law of the land and the Constitution of India, not to any people, party or government. It is incumbent upon the government to provide him all encouragement, so he will be able to become a public servant in the true sense of the expression.'

They also gave a direction orally that the judgement should be implemented within twelve weeks. The government had been asked to treat the entire period of Jaiswal's absence as duty. Not only for service purposes, but he had to be given all pay, and allowances that he had been deprived of.

The date was 24 January 1984, two days before Republic Day, and roughly the time that the astrologer, Panditji, had predicted that the sun would shine again. Jaiswal was thrilled beyond measure. But the story didn't end there. Twelve weeks came and went and the court order had not been implemented.

A couple more weeks passed and still he did not hear from the government. He then went to the Ministry of

Home Affairs to chase up on his order. They directed him to the joint secretary of police, who blandly told Jaiswal, 'Yes, we know that. We are pursuing the order.'

'But, sir, the Supreme Court has ordered that within twelve weeks it should be passed. It is fourteen weeks already,' Jaiswal protested.

'What does the Supreme Court know about our difficulties? We are examining it. Be patient.'

'It is not that, sir. I am not a party to it any more. It is between the Supreme Court and the MHA now. Tomorrow, I am going to file another petition in the Supreme Court to ask why the order has not been implemented in twelve weeks.'

'Why are you all the time threatening with the name of the Supreme Court?'

'I am not threatening, sir. I have been driven to the wall. I have fought the case and won it and I have come back. I have a wife and two children to feed. Now, even after I have won the case, implementation is being difficult. I have no choice but to go back to the court, since I can't get fair play from the government. Sorry to have wasted your time and disturbed you.'

He excused himself and walked out of North Block. As he was going down the wide stairs, the PA of the joint secretary came running behind him, shouting, 'Mr Jaiswal, Mr Jaiswal.' Jaiswal turned around and the PA asked him, 'Are you living in Delhi?'

'Yes.'

'Can you give me your phone number?'

He gave the phone number of his father-in-law's residence.

The next morning, at around 10 a.m., there was a phone call for him with the message that Jaiswal had to get to the Ministry of Home Affairs immediately. Chaturvedi was still the home secretary, but he was going to retire and M.K. Wali was about to replace him. The PA explained that when the Supreme Court order came, Chaturvedi did not agree to sign the re-instatement. When it was pointed out that it was a Supreme Court order, he had exploded, 'Let Wali come and do it. I am not going to.'

But they had persuaded him and he had finally agreed and just that morning he had signed it. The order said Jaiswal had to join within three days. He was stunned.

'But I have to go back to Gorakhpur and pick up my luggage. How do I get to Tamil Nadu in three days? From Delhi to Gorakhpur, it is eight hundred kilometres, and from there then to Madurai for field training, about eighteen hundred kilometres and no direct trains,' Jaiswal pointed out. What was he to do?

Then he was told, 'Ah, I cannot help you there, Mr Jaiswal. Here is the order. What you do and how you do it is up to you.'

19

Beginner's Luck

Before you are posted as an IPS officer, there is training, which lasts nine to ten months. You are attached as a sub-inspector for a while, a traffic police officer for a while, and you learn the language of the state you are allotted. In Jaiswal's case, the language was Tamil. He conducted village visits and familiarized himself with the police standing orders of Tamil Nadu.

It was all in capsule form. They could make you in charge of a police station for a month, a traffic constable for a week, then you would be inspector of a circle, with three police stations under you, you would go for night patrol with the beat policemen. It was a period when you got a feel of every aspect of policing. For Jaiswal, there was nine months of it in Madurai. By 1985, Jaiswal was ready to be posted with independent charge.

In Madurai, he stayed in a constable's quarters, a very small accommodation, what was called Type Four quarters.

The government provided him with a motorcycle, a Royal Enfield Bullet, with the instruction that he was not to ride the motorcycle. He could only sit as a pillion rider. They provided a rider. The idea was that if there was an accident, the assistant superintendent of police should not be liable. The rider took him anywhere he wanted to go. It was a bit strange. If he had to run an errand, he had to use the rider.

Jaiswal had become famous or notorious in the service because of the entire saga of being dismissed from service and reinstated. Hence, most of the senior officers avoided meeting him if they could help it. His superintendent, the Madurai SP, R.N. Sawani, who was three years his senior, for example, always avoided addressing the new assistant superintendent of police by name.

'ASP Training, follow me,' he would order.

'ASP Training, be in my office at nine tomorrow morning.'

Every Sunday, Jaiswal would be required to write a weekly diary, encapsulating the week's work. It had to be in a printed form. You got one form, but it was never enough. You had to attach A4 sheets to get through the entire week. Jaiswal didn't have secretarial assistance, and neither did he own a typewriter, so he wrote these reports with the pen, in longhand. Then these were handed over to the SP. Jaiswal wrote the first weekly diary and he went to Sawani with it, saluted him, and handed it over to him. Sawani looked at it, flipped through it, kept it aside, and dismissed Jaiswal, who went back home. Barely half an hour later, a motorcycle rider came with a tapal (a letter). It turned out to be a memo from the SP. It said, the ASP Training, is hereby directed not to staple his weekly diary but to punch a hole and tie it with a thread.

It was a bit strange. Sawani could have told him the same thing then and there when he had handed him the report. The following week Jaiswal submitted the weekly diary and this time he took care to punch a hole through the pages and tied them all with a thread. The next day, on Monday, Jaiswal went to Sawani's office, saluted him, and handed over the report. SP Sawani accepted the report, and Jaiswal stood, waiting to see if he had anything to say. Again, Sawani dismissed Jaiswal, and he went away.

After an hour, a rider came and handed him another memo. It said, ASP Training to ensure that the pages of the weekly diary are of the same size. Apparently, one of the sheets of paper was a little wider or longer than the others. Jaiswal had used whatever paper was available when he was writing the report. Jaiswal thought about it, and decided maybe it was the police culture, and he had to adhere.

Jaiswal was posted as assistant superintendent of police, Ambasamudram subdivision, in Tirunelveli district. This was in 1985. His knowledge of Tamil Nadu was poor. He looked at the map of Tirunelveli. He assumed that if the ASP was posted in a subdivision, the deputy collector also must be there. To his surprise, he found the deputy collector in a town called Cheranmahadevi. Ambasamudram was not mentioned on the map. He made enquiries and found that though the deputy collector sat in Cheranmahadevi, the

ASP's office, called the subdivisional police office, was in Ambasamudram, about fifteen kilometres away.

Jaiswal had a rider called Bajan, short for Bajendran. He told Bajan to find out which bus went to Ambasamudram. Jaiswal couldn't take his wife and children and his parents, who, on hearing that their son had got his first posting, had joined him in Madurai. All of them lived in that two-room small Type Four constables' quarters. The plan was Jaiswal would go and find accommodation in Ambasamudram and then get them there. He thought it would take a week or so.

Bajendran found out that there was a direct bus from Madurai to Ambasamudram. Jaiswal wouldn't have to change in Tirunelveli. Bajendran also said he would send a message to the Tirunelveli SP as well as the Ambasamudram DSP that the ASP was coming to join duty. Jaiswal said, 'Bajendran, don't do that. I will reach there and show them the order. There is no need to make a fuss of it.' A copy of the order would have gone there as a matter of routine, and there was no need to announce his arrival in any other manner. The bus passed, coincidentally, near the quarters where he lived, and Bajendran had arranged for the bus to make a small halt to let the ASP board it when it passed by the quarters.

With a holdall and a small suitcase which held his belongings, Jaiswal boarded the bus. Both the holdall and suitcase went on top of the bus. He was comfortably seated in a corner seat.

Tirunelveli was a three-hour bus ride away from

Madurai. It was half past eight in the morning. By about eleven fifteen, the bus reached Tirunelveli. At the bus stand stood a police jeep and a driver. A uniformed constable boarded the bus. The constable looked around and went away, and the bus continued its journey. From Tirunelveli, Ambasamudram was an hour away. As the bus neared Ambasamudram, Jaiswal called the conductor and asked him how far the DSP's office was from the bus stand.

The conductor said, 'Don't get down at the Ambasamudram bus stand. This bus goes to Vickramasinghapuram. That is the last stop for this bus. The DSP's office is right on the main road, less than two kilometres away. I will stop the bus there, and you can get down.'

The bus moved again, and they reached Ambasamudram. Jaiswal saw many policemen around the bus stand, some with their ceremonial cross-belts. There were at least twenty or twenty-five policemen at the bus stand. A couple of policemen boarded the bus, looked around, got down again, and the bus moved on. Jaiswal thought it unusual that in Tamil Nadu, police should enter buses at the main bus stands. It had not been in any of the capsules of training. Nor did he remember seeing it in the police standing orders. A couple of kilometres down the road, the conductor halted the bus and indicated that Jaiswal should get off. His holdall and suitcase were brought down. Holding them in either hand, Jaiswal walked into the DSP's office, which was just across the road.

It looked deserted. Someone came out of the office and Jaiswal asked him, 'Is DSP sir in the office?'

'DSP aiyyah Tirunelveli pointanga, SP avara parka.' (DSP has gone to Tirunelveli to meet the SP.)

Jaiswal kept standing there with the suitcase and the holdall in his hands. He asked the man why the office was empty.

'Inikki puthu ASP varaaru.' (Today the new ASP is coming.)

'Naanthaan puthu ASP' (I am the new ASP), Jaiswal told him.

The man, who turned out to be the camp clerk, immediately relieved Jaiswal of the suitcase and the holdall and ushered him inside, and showed him to a chair, all the time saying, 'Sir, sir, sir. Adada! Yellarum ungale varaverthukkku bus stand poirkirrango.' (But everyone has gone to the bus stand to receive you.) Didn't they see you? Everybody has gone there to the bus stand.)

The camp clerk got on the wireless and the telephone to announce that the new ASP had arrived. Bajendran had sent the particulars of the bus Jaiswal was travelling in both to the SP in Tirunelveli and the DSP in Ambasamudram. The SP in Tirunelveli had sent a jeep to the bus station with the instruction that Jaiswal should get off the bus, so that he could meet him before Jaiswal reported for duty. The DSP, meanwhile, had corralled the staff from the nearby police stations to put together a police party to receive him properly when the bus arrived at the Ambasamudram bus stand.

As the camp clerk was speaking on the wireless, there

suddenly came a message, 'Papakudi para pesarein, Papakudi para pesarein. (I am the para-constable in Papakudi.) I am alone at the police station. People from the village are saying that a man has murdered his wife and is taking her body to cremate it. The villagers wanted the police to stop the man from burning his wife.'

The camp clerk called across to the new ASP, 'Sir, there is a murder case, there is a murder case at Papakudi police station.' The new ASP sat there, nonplussed. He didn't know what to do. He was the ASP now, and he didn't even know where Papakudi was. There were no policemen around him, only the camp clerk. He did not know what instruction to give or to whom.

In his anxiety to do something quickly, Jaiswal snatched the wireless from the camp clerk's hand and, in the process, it somehow got switched off. A heavy silence descended. The camp clerk kept looking at the new ASP silently and a little strangely.

Call it a bizarre stroke of luck, but after the para police constable of Papakudi shouted his message, Jaiswal heard the typical sound of a Bullet motorcycle thumping outside the police station, and he rushed to stop the motorcycle. It turned out to be an inspector who happened to pass that way. The inspector had slowed down seeing the agitated crowd outside the Papakudi police station. The para police constable explained the problem to the inspector. He, in turn, took a villager on his pillion, rode quickly to the village. When he reached the man had already set his wife's body on fire. The inspector got villagers to haul water from the nearest well and had it poured over the burning body. It was out of his jurisdiction, and there was nothing else he could do.

Within an hour, Jaiswal was able to reach the spot after the police came back from the bus stand. Only her hair and a portion of the face had been burned, along with some portions of her waist and hands. Jaiswal sent the body for post-mortem. The arrest was made. But for that inspector passing Pappakudi coincidentally, Jaiswal would have been taken to task. Beginner's luck, you think?

20

9th Battalion

Eight months into his posting as assistant superintendent of police in Ambasamudram, Jaiswal was due for promotion. There were five policemen in his batch and the other four had become superintendents of police heading various districts. Jaiswal received an order saying he was posted as commandant, 9th Battalion, Manimuthar, which was adjacent, less than eleven kilometres southwest. The morning papers announced the posting, then the wireless message came, saying he had to take charge immediately.

The office staff were gloomy. One of them, a head constable, reacted to the news saying, 'Aiyyah ungalakku Battalion kuduthutango' (You have been given a battalion only), implying he had been relegated to a secondary position while all his batchmates had become SPs in Ramnad, Madurai, etc.

Jaiswal felt low, but he put on his uniform and set out in his jeep to take charge. At the address given in Manimuthar, there stood a line of barracks and buildings, all empty and in disuse. Thinking there must be some mistake, he kept driving around so he could find the commandant's office and take charge from the outgoing commandant. He couldn't find a single person anywhere.

Strange.

A battalion usually consisted of seven companies of people, nearly eight hundred people. Sometimes it would be eight hundred and fifty depending on extra duties which may be attached. Here, he could see no one, not a soul.

Turning a corner, he came upon four or five constables who were strolling. They looked relaxed. Jaiswal stopped his jeep and asked them, 'Where is the office of the commandant of the 9th Battalion?'

One among them was a head constable. He said, 'But Tamil Nadu has only eight battalions. There is no 9th Battalion. How come you are asking for the 9th Battalion? Please check if you have the battalion right.'

Jaiswal took out the posting order. There, written very clearly in Roman letters, 'IXth Battalion, and VIIIth and IXth', couldn't be more different from each other. There was no confusion that it was the 9th Battalion.

'Which battalion is this? These buildings?'

'This is the 6th Battalion. But the battalion has gone to Delhi. They have gone to guard Tihar Jail. The battalion is now empty.'

'Then what are you doing here? Which battalion are you?' Jaiswal asked.

'Sir, we belong to the 3rd Battalion, in Manimuthar, which is about two kilometres from here. We have come for sentry duty to guard the 6th Battalion's buildings and properties, the fans, the light fittings.'

Jaiswal asked for directions to the 3rd Battalion and set off there. The commandant was Mr Mariappan. He entered his office and saluted him, an elderly person, and said, 'I've been posted as Commandant 9th Battalion, but there seems to be no such battalion.'

Mariappan looked at him and said, 'Show me your papers. This is the 3rd Battalion, and there are only eight battalions in Tamil Nadu. There must be a mistake.'

Jaiswal sought permission to use his phone and called the DGP's office. The DGP was Mr Ravindran, who had been in the Intelligence Bureau for a long time and he had a very non-uniform approach to policing. His PA connected him to the DGP who came on the line and pronounced jovially, 'Congratulations Jaiswal, you've got your promotion.'

'Yes, sir, thank you! But I have been posted as commandant of the 9th Battalion, but there is no such battalion. I am perplexed.'

'Jaiswal, I know there is no 9th Battalion, but now that we have posted you, we have made a beginning. Already the recruitment has been done. You take over the 6th Battalion campus. Soon you will be starting their training. You will be getting not eight hundred people but a thousand recruits, or maybe a few more. We are recruiting for other battalions also, but we will send those to the 9th for training.'

Mariappan volunteered to help. He said he would loan some manpower.

The commandant's residence, which had been vacant for three or four months, was spruced up, and Jaiswal and his family moved in.

The single-storey house had three bedrooms, with nearly half an acre of the compound around it. Beyond the compound lay a mango grove. There were four hundred mango trees there, neatly planted, standing like soldiers in camouflage ready for inspection in a parade. You could tell when the mango season began because a huge variety of birds descended on the trees. The parrots were the noisiest. They were noisier when they were gorging on fruits. So did monkeys and bears. On one occasion, they counted seven bears trooping in, and once, even a tiger arrived, although it did not come for the mangoes.

The head of the massive Manimuthar dam lay less than two hundred yards away. Curiously, there were no stray dogs in Manimuthar, not even one, and when Jaiswal asked about it, he was told that leopards came and took them away. In the silence of the night, dogs invariably gave their locations away by barking, and the leopards had no difficulty finding them.

The commandant's bungalow had a wall painted white on the front and the rest was light barbed wire fencing. Beyond the fence was a bit of a rocky patch and then there was the Thamarabarani river, which was almost dry because of the damming. When the water was released, the river brimmed and flowed swiftly by the commandant's residence. On quiet nights, over the sounds of the forests, they could hear the river gurgle by.

Pressing down upon them, all around them, was the Kalakad-Mundanthurai Tiger Reserve. In the distance, the hills stood like sentries.

Mariappan also gave Jaiswal's house a sentry, till the 9th Battalion was formed.

One day, the sentry reported that behind the fencing, someone had spotted a big python. They went to see it and couldn't find it. One of the recruits was from the Irula tribe (who specialize in snake catching) and he said if it had been spotted there the snake must be familiar with the area and would come back again to rest in the sun; pythons were territorial.

Within two days, the Irula boy returned and said the python was back, now lying on a rock very near the fence. Neelam was alarmed. She pointed out that the children often played in the compound. The assistant commandant, who was a good shot, offered to put a bullet into it. The Irula boy interjected, saying the snake was harmless. While they were talking, the python slithered off the rocks and slipped smoothly into the Thamarabarani without a ripple. The very next day, the Irula boy came back and said the python was there again, and if he could have six or seven people and a gunny bag, he would do the job.

There were many volunteers. Jaiswal went and stood at the fence and saw the lot take a long detour to get to the rock. The Irula boy said the vibrations caused by so many feet on the rock would make the snake move but the snake didn't, and even as Jaiswal watched, they let out a cry and pounced upon the big, fat snake, each grabbing a part of it, with the Irula boy leading the charge. And in some time, they came holding aloft the snake with the Irula boy holding the head as if it were some coveted and hard-won trophy. The party came to the front of the residence. It must have been easily over four metres long.

They laid the python down on the ground and each of them sat on the snake to hold it down. They were going to take the snake to the forest in a gunny bag and leave it there. The children were too frightened to touch the python, but the python was made to pose for photographs and then was bundled into a gunny bag and it was a wonder how such a big snake would fit so snuggly, so quietly into it. The python was given a ride in the commandant's jeep deep into the forest where it would hopefully make another home.

The spillover water from the Manimuthar dam formed deep pools at many places and even the release tank which was more than a hundred metres long and equally wide with deep green water was abundant with all sorts of fish. Every evening at five o'clock, they went there with angling rods, stood near the dam on a small platform and threw lines into the water below. Normally three lines with live bait consisting of mannu puzhu (earthworms) were used and by the time the third line was thrown, the first line would be quivering with a fish at the end of it.

The first fifteen days were all administrative work. There was no telephone, only a wireless set. There was no one to talk to. Messages came either by telegram or wireless. After about twenty days, the people started to trickle in, assistant commandant, deputy commandant, and the recruits.

The recruits had to be given rigorous parade and physical training. The morning parades began. There were some small capsule courses for law, social sciences, and behaviour. That was when the commandant ran afoul of the police hierarchy.

He talked freely to the recruits, but the other senior staff were uneasy. An assistant commandant would not allow a sub-inspector to be even seated in his presence and here was a commandant who was talking away, almost as equals, sitting side by side. If he went somewhere in his jeep and he saw some from the battalion headed down the road, the commandant gave them a lift. If he was walking somewhere, he would walk with them.

He did not like the distances between the ranks, and treated them exactly as he would have treated IPS trainees. It was unthinkable for the other officer ranks that their commandant would stop his jeep and take a constable who had been injured and drop him off at the infirmary. One of the deputy commandants said, 'Sir, don't treat them like officers. Otherwise, they will become useless and sit on top of your head.'

People had to be hired for the various tasks to be done in the battalion premises. It was up to the commandant to hire them. One day, there was a message that thirty sweepers had to be recruited. Another day, they would be hiring gardeners. What were the criteria? Because they would become government servants, advertisements were given. There were Manthiram and his wife. Accompanied by a rickety child, they came to become sweepers, both of them. For two days, while they waited, they lived under a tree. The only criterion the commandant had was to give the job to the poorest of the poor.

Occasionally, constables ran away. If they didn't return in three weeks' time, they would be declared 'deserters' and struck off the rolls. One day, the deputy commandant said that thirteen people had been absent for many days and ought to be struck off the rolls.

'Let's not do it,' the commandant responded. 'Getting a government job is not easy. Send a couple of inspectors to their home addresses and talk to their parents or relatives to find out why they left and then come and tell me.'

All the thirteen were rounded up and were brought to the commandant's office along with their parents. Some of them said they were scared of the havildar, some were bullied by so and so. Some said that the food in the mess was making them sick. Jaiswal said he'd look into all these matters. And they continued their training.

However, training to be constables didn't guarantee the means to an income until they were recruited. Now they were getting a decent income. Jaiswal came across instances of training officers taking a cut off the trainees' salaries in exchange for them, not giving them extra drill or punishment.

There were two squads that were targeted. One was the weak squad, which consisted of those who were not able to come up to the required standard. They were given extra drill. The other was the punishment squad, trainees who came late to a class or drill, or were not in the prescribed attire, or those found loitering beyond permissible hours. The punishment squad was always a good source for extortion. If a havildar did not get his bottle of liquor from a recruit, as expected, he would find some fault and put the person on the punishment squad.

Jaiswal did not want confrontation in each and every case. He chose to handle both the weak squad and the punishment squad himself. If, say, two hundred people had been singled out for punishment, he went to the field and took the extra drill and the punishment tasks in the afternoon and the evening, mentioning that the punishment was not meant for their humiliation, but to ensure they didn't repeat their mistakes and they learnt from them.

One tonne of rice was cooked daily in the mess. The recruits worked out a lot and so they ate a lot. Jaiswal figured the meal plan: what was required was a heap of rice, sambar, a heap of rice, rasam, a heap of rice, moru, buttermilk, and poriyal and pappadam and urugai, pickle, other things that went along with it. Non-vegetarian, too. Because of the Manimuthar dam, fish were plentiful, loads of variety, cheap. They relied more on fish rather than chicken or mutton, which were expensive. Rohu and katla, both freshwater fish, were sold those days at twenty-five rupees per kg.

Most of the battalion liked the taste of karuvadu, dried fish, in their sambar. The proportion was one to one and a half kg of karuvadu for about a hundred people. It was a flavouring agent, the dried fish. A touch of karuvadu turned sambar into a kind of fish curry.

It was the recruits' money. They paid the mess fees. But there was cutting and pilferage going on within. Jaiswal made it a point to eat one meal a day in the mess. There were eight messes, one for each company. Each company's mess was independent but stood near each other. Two small buildings and some tents housed these messes. When it was not raining, they ate in the open. Jaiswal took to eating in the messes, randomly.

As soon as he entered, they would bring him a plate to taste. He would push it away. There was a line where constables stood and each carried a plate and when their turn came at the head of the queue they were served from behind the counter and they went and sat down and ate. Jaiswal would wait for a constable to fill his thali and then ask him to give him the thali, and ask him to pick up another thali and serve himself, while he ate what the constable had been served, sitting among them. This had a dramatic effect on the quality of food.

Swimming was made compulsory because the dam was right there and the wide Thamarabarani river too. There would be intensive swimming training for those who didn't know how to swim. The battalion sat by the side of a tiger reserve. Jaiswal had studied in a Sainik School, surviving hostel life from class eight, and had been briefly in the NDA, learning all the drills and the survival skills in those years. So, he made survival skills a part of their training.

DGP Ravindran tasked that the first commando unit of the Tamil Nadu Police be raised in the 9th Battalion.

In the second month of the training, it occurred to Jaiswal that all should go for a picnic from Manimuthar to Courtallam. The drive via Ambasamudram and through Kadayam to Courtallam Falls on the Chittar river was very scenic. On the left side of the road, the Western Ghats began to rise, and on the right, the endless lush green paddy fields.

Jaiswal wanted to announce that they would go for a long march from Manimuthar to Courtallam, a distance of forty-two kilometres. Midway breakfast at Kadayam, lunch at Courtallam, tea back at Kadayam and dinner at Manimuthar. Roughly, he worked out that to walk eighty-four kilometres it would take fourteen to fifteen hours. He did not take into consideration the tiredness which would catch up after having walked about thirty to forty kilometres.

Initially his officers objected, saying it would be too long a march, many would not be able to make it, that among officers who were trainers there were some older persons as well. So, it was decided all the trucks with the 9th Battalion and buses would be deployed for carrying food and for people who were not able to walk or for whatever distance they were able to walk.

The next day at the parade, he announced there would be a picnic, those who could walk could walk and those who for some reason could not would take the bus, have lunch at Courtallam, bathe in the falls and come back. There were looks of surprise at this and a loud murmuring began. Jaiswal asked those who did not want to come to raise their hands and very few hands went up, about a dozen. They would go on Saturday, for on Sunday Courtallam would be very crowded. If they began the march after morning tea at five then they would be back for dinner at nine or so in the night.

Jaiswal too took to walking. Up to Kadayam, which was twenty-five kilometres away, the walk was comfortable. At Kadayam, the trucks were waiting with sundal and boiled eggs and tea. From Kadayam, when he started walking, he realized he was faltering. In another ten kilometres, both his hips started aching.

That was when the driver of the jeep which was following him noticed his unsteady gait and asked him to get in. Neelam and the two children were already in the jeep. They reached Courtallam by jeep and by the time the recruits got there, the sumptuous smell of biryani was spreading all over like a fragrant blanket. They spent some time in the water and realized that the more time they spent there, the less time they had to get back. Many of the recruits were sleepy after the heavy meal of mutton biryani. The walk back began.

Jaiswal drove back and waited at Manimuthar. By six in the evening they should have reached Kadayam to have tea. But not many turned up at the appointed time. Among the more resourceful and imaginative of the lot, some caught buses and some thumbed down passing trucks to reach

Ambasamudram. By nine in the evening when dinner was to be served, about eight hundred people had arrived. There were still more than a hundred out there on the road, on their way back. A jeep was sent to find the rest. Quite a number of them were still walking and dinner was kept hot for them as well. Around half past eleven in the night, the commandant found that except for fourteen or fifteen, all others had arrived after nearly twenty hours.

For the stragglers, a vehicle was sent out again. Some two kilometres from the battalion, they found all the fourteen people sitting on some rocks by the road. They were resting. They were urged to get into the vehicle. They declined saying that they wanted to complete the task by walking all the way back. Even if it took an hour or two to walk the final two kilometres.

A month after this, either June or July, suddenly, electricity went off during the night. Howling winds roamed outside. The monsoon was well on its way. Jaiswal went out to see if the fuse in the residence had blown. He stepped outside and a guard, seeing him, came out and told Jaiswal that a big tree had fallen on the electric wire that led to the residence and it had snapped.

Jaiswal knew it would take time before some help arrived, and for the electricity to be restored. He went back home to try and sleep for what remained of the night. It must have been 4–4.30 a.m. and he had to be out by seven. The fan started moving after about half an hour. Surprised, he went outside and saw scores of 9th Battalion trainees busy at work chopping the branches of the tree. Among the constabulary, there were electricians as well, and they had climbed up the poles with the wire retrieved from the tree and had connected it again.

One morning, from the quarter guard opposite his residence, where all the weapons were stored, the commandant heard sounds weeping, and went outside to check. He heard more sounds weeping. He went up to the guardroom and saw the guard weeping. He asked him, 'What's the matter? Why is there weeping going on?' The guard continued to cry. It was very strange.

He saw sub-inspector Kochukrishnan walking up to him and asked him what was happening here. Kochukrishnan looked at Jaiswal and began to cry, too. Through his tears he said, 'Aiyyah va maathitango, neenga SP aitingo, Tuticorin la.' (You have been transferred as SP, Tuticorin.)

The news had hit them hard. He didn't believe that he had built such an emotional rapport. It was not because he did anything more than he had to, but they simply didn't expect to be treated so well and fairly.

As he began to prepare for his transfer, Kochukrishnan came and told him that the recruits wanted to give him a farewell gift. Jaiswal said he could not accept a gift from them. Two constables had come with him.

One of them said, 'If we give you a gift of fifty naya paise, will you accept it?' It would be churlish to refuse a gift of fifty paise, and the commandant said, yes, that he would accept. They gave him an Allwyn automatic watch. Each of them had contributed fifty paise. Jaiswal still has the watch, and it works.

In return, Jaiswal bought an HMT watch, HMT Sooraj, which was in those days a coveted possession. It was to be given to the best cadet when this batch of the 9th Battalion passed out.

He would feel the benefit of this early posting long afterwards. In 1989, he was posted in the Intelligence Bureau in New Delhi and had to find accommodation. His family was temporarily housed in a small guest house. Any IAS or IPS officer posted to Delhi would have to apply for quarters at Nirman Bhavan. Fifteen days afterwards, a transit accommodation near Pragati Maidan was provided. It was already a fortnight after the application was made and Jaiswal went to Nirman Bhavan to get the allotment of the transit quarters. When he reached there, he was told that the application was not traceable. They asked him to give a fresh application.

This meant another fifteen days at the guest house. This was frustrating. He filled out the form again, submitted it, and walked to the IB office on Akbar Road. The Vice President's residence stood just before Akbar Road. As he was walked past it, he noticed that all the sentries at the Vice President's house stood at attention with a snap of their rifles and emphatic stomping of their feet. Jaiswal kept walking and thinking that some guest must be going to the VP's house.

Then behind him some constables came running,

shouting, 'Aiyyah, aiyyah,' and he turned back, and they said, 'Aiyyah, namma 9th Battalion constable.' (Sir, I am a constable from the 9th Battalion.)

Jaiswal asked them what they were doing there.

Guarding the Vice President, they said. The battalion had moved to guard Tihar Jail, and a company had been detailed to the Vice President's house.

They asked him where he was going, and Jaiswal pointed out that he was going to Akbar Road, a few hundred yards away. They said, 'Vendam aiyyah.' (No, sir. We will drop you.)

He could not see any vehicle, but soon a fifty-two-seater bus turned up, and they said, 'Aiyyah, yerungo.' (Please get in, sir.)

It was payback time for all the pickups and drops he had done.

The sentry at the IB office was surprised. The sub-inspector came along and asked where his quarters were, and Jaiswal told him that he was having difficulty getting accommodation. 'Yenge, aiyyah? Nirman Bhavan liya?' (Where, sir? In Nirman Bhavan?)

Jaiswal said that the matter was stuck in Nirman Bhavan. The sub-inspector said, 'Kavala padanthingo, aiyah. Naan senchu kotuthooduren.' (Don't worry, sir. I will handle it. Just give me the details.)

The very next day, Jaiswal got his allotment order for his accommodation at Pragati Maidan through the Tamil network in Nirman Bhavan.

When Jaiswal came back to Chennai in 2003, he was

in bad shape emotionally. Cancer was taking his daughter, Mini, away. He was living in the Wallajah Road IG quarters, and was yet to be given a posting. There was no paraphernalia without a posting. He did not have a car. He was going to fetch provisions in the morning. He was not wearing his uniform. There was nothing to suggest that he was a policeman. He walked out to Mount Road and was waiting at the edge for the traffic to thin so he could run across the road, cross the divider, and run to the other side of the road, dodging traffic as he went.

A traffic head constable came up, went up to the divider and stopped the traffic coming on both sides of the road, and after the traffic had come to a halt, with his wireless set in his hand, he walked up and said, 'Aiyyah, cross pannungo.' (Please cross the road.)

Jaiswal was taken aback, but he crossed the road and the head constable crossed along with him, and once they were on the other side of the road, Jaiswal asked him why he had done it, and the constable saluted him and said, 'Aiyyah, naan 9th Battalion constable.' (I am from the 9th Battalion.)

In 2007, Manu, Jaiswal's son, was due to get married. Somebody had suggested they go to a big, well-known saree shop in T. Nagar. They were upstairs on the first floor, but he had absolutely nothing to do, and was loitering around, while Neelam was doing the saree selection. His role was minimal in this, close to no role, in fact. As he wandered idly here and there, someone came up to him. He introduced himself as the manager of the shop, and then he folded his hands, and kept saying, 'Sir, it is beyond my power, sir. It is beyond my power. Please believe me, it is beyond my power.'

'What power are you talking about?'

'The maximum rebate I can give you is twenty-five per cent. Fifty per cent I cannot give, sir.'

Jaiswal was stunned. 'But I have not asked for any rebate. Not even one per cent rebate. What is all this?'

'You are Anoop Jaiswal?'

'Yes, I am Anoop Jaiswal.'

'Sir, there is a policeman standing at the counter downstairs, threatening us that we have to give you fifty per cent rebate. I have been told that if we don't give that, not one vehicle will be allowed to stop or stand in front of this shop.'

'Who is that fellow? I never asked anybody to threaten you. Please pardon me. I have not told anyone to do this. I don't want any concession or rebate.'

Jaiswal walked down with him and saw a head constable standing there and asked him, 'How do you explain your behaviour?'

'Aiyyah, naan 9th Battalion constable,' he said, snapping into a salute. Jaiswal told the manager again, 'I do not want any concession. Please charge the full amount. I don't want to go away feeling I have misused my authority.'

Now the manager interrupted. 'No, sir. We will give you twenty-five per cent concession.' Finally, Jaiswal agreed to take a ten per cent concession.

The 9th Battalion followed Anoop Jaiswal like a faithful

shadow. Long after he left Manimuthar, Manimuthar refused to leave him. He knew he would go back there again.

Long ago he had bought three acres of land near the battalion, dreaming that some day he would build an ashram there, a stone's throw from the mango grove with the parrots, and the garden where butterflies hung heavy in the air between the flowers, there, by the Manimuthar dam, amidst the teak trees, nestling in the shade, the wind rustling through the leaves and the tall grass all around, and not far away the clack of the drill sounds drifting from the 9th Battalion parade grounds.

As each day passes, Anoop Jaiswal knows, he knows deep within himself, that he is moving one step closer to that day.

Acknowledgements

It is far easier to write a book than to have it published, however good you might think it has turned out be, especially in terms of its relevance.

If your work is rooted in reality, and every character who lives, breathes or dies in its pages is as real as real can be, it is generally true that the writing would not have been possible without help, particularly if you were not present for all the action that you have described in the book. Here I would like to acknowledge the two categories of people who *Tuticorin* possible: those who ensured that it was written in the manner it has been, and those who made it take the shape and appearance you now hold in your hands.

This would not have been possible, first of all, if Anoop Jaiswal had not been convinced that these were tales worth telling, and if his family had not encouraged him to share the stories of the people who shaped his life. I would like to thank Neelam Jaiswal for opening their home to me and for putting up with my inquisitiveness. If there is a solid bedrock to the book, it is because Manu Jaiswal preserved the records of his father's life: whether it was a six-paragraph report on page five of the Madurai edition of the *Indian Express,* dated 24 October 1988, or a picture from 3 March 1988 of Antony Mookan being presented with a livelihood grant by the officials of the State Bank of India. He didn't let the terrible floods of December 2015 – when the Jaiswals' home was almost fully immersed in water as the Chembarambakkam reservoir flowed freely all over the city – claim them, a fate that was meted out to much else that was in the house. And to Swasthi, Jaiswal's granddaughter, without whose laughter and encouragement her grandmother would not have made me a different soup for each day that I visited them.

I gratefully acknowledge the warm and welcoming hospitality of K.S.P.S. Kannan of Tuticorin, and that of his wife, Meenakshi, for being such wonderful hosts and storytellers. Among other things, they gave additional insights into life in Tuticorin in the eighties. I am deeply grateful to Kalyani Raja of Ambasamudram and his wife, Subhadra, for their encouragement and for preparing a meal I will never forget for its sumptuousness, taste and spread. I would be remiss if I did not mention Sub-Inspector (retired) S. Kannan who was with us for most of the trip to help me navigate the geography, as well as some of the events in this book.

It must be said that in the unpredictable path to publication, there are those who recognize a manuscript for what it is worth and guide it unerringly to publishers, and there are those who have missed seeing the wood for the trees. I have to put on the record the unstinting faith, enthusiasm, professionalism and speed with which The Suitable Agency – and here I want to mention Hemali Sodhi and Ambar Sahil Chatterjee and their ringing endorsement of the manuscript – steered it to a welcoming home. I would like to thank Juggernaut for its spirit of adventure and core values in publishing, and Devanghsu Datta for his serendipitous faith in this book and the encouragement and clarity that he has given it.

I thank my daughter Rudraa Abirami Sudarshan for putting this book on the map, as it were, and for her patience.

Finally, there is thing called the angel's share ... Apparently, when alcoholic drinks like whiskey or brandy are aged and distilled in barrels, some of the spirits evaporate; it is said that the portion that dissipates belongs to the angels – a sincere token of our appreciation. I raise a hearty toast to all those unseen and unnamed, mostly inadvertently, who partook in the making of this book. Usually, the angel's share is considered to be anything between two to five per cent. Here I can emphatically say that it has been much more, practically unquantifiable. And, here's, especially, to Tuticorin!

A Note on the Author

V. Sudarshan is a journalist and the author of the non-fiction narratives, *Dead End: The Minister, the CBI and the Murder That Wasn't*; *Adrift: A True Story of Survival at Sea* and *Anatomy of an Abduction: How the Indian Hostages in Iraq Were Freed*. He also writes short stories. He lives in Mumbai.

To download the app scan the QR Code
with a QR scanner app